Native Actors and Filmmakers

VISUAL STORYTELLERS

Gary Robinson

7th
GENERATION

NATIVE VOICES
Summertown, TN

Library of Congress Cataloging-in-Publication Data available upon request

We chose to print this title on paper certified by The Forest Stewardship Council®
(FSC®), a global, not-for-profit organization dedicated to the promotion of responsible
forest management worldwide.

7th Generation,
an imprint of Book Publishing Company
PO Box 99
Summertown, TN 38483
888-260-8458
bookpubco.com
nativevoicesbooks.com

Printed in the United States of America

ISBN: 978-1-939053-31-2

Photo credits found on page 122.

26 25 24 23 22 21   1 2 3 4 5 6 7 8 9

T his work is dedicated to the memory of four people who were early Native trailblazers in the field of entertainment and media production: film festival pioneer Mike Smith (Fort Peck Sioux; 1951–2018), producer-director Phil Lucas (Choctaw; 1942–2007), Native entertainment activist Bob Hicks (Muscogee-Creek; 1934–2014), and Native actor Will Sampson (Muscogee-Creek; 1933–1987).

Mike founded the American Indian Film Institute (AIFI) and American Indian Film Festival (AIFF) in 1975, providing a much-needed means of bringing Native perspectives and stories to mainstream audiences through film and television. The AIFF, still operating from San Francisco, is the oldest competitive showcase for Native filmmakers and actors in North America.

Phil (my close friend and mentor) was all about telling the true stories of the struggles and accomplishments of Native peoples on film and video and correcting the negative stereotypes often depicted in movies and television. During a long career, he created many groundbreaking projects. In 1979, Phil wrote, coproduced, and codirected a five-part documentary series called *Images of Indians* for PBS. In 1986, he produced and directed *The Honor of All*, a dramatic re-creation of a Canadian tribe's recovery from the devastating effects of alcohol.

Beginning in 1979, Bob Hicks was a leading voice advocating for Native Americans in Hollywood, raising awareness of issues facing Native professionals within the entertainment industry. He founded First Americans in the Arts, an organization created to recognize, honor, and promote American Indian participation in the entertainment industry, incorporating film, television, music, and theater.

Muscogee-Creek actor Will Sampson, best known for his role as Chief Bromden in 1975's *One Flew Over the Cuckoo's Nest*, served as the host and narrator for the PBS documentary television series *Images of Indians*. In 1983, he founded and served on the board of directors of the American Indian Registry for the Performing Arts, which published a directory of Native actors, producers, directors, and crew talent that was distributed to members of the Los Angeles production profession. (I was privileged to be included in that directory one year.)

All four broke ground in the fields of entertainment and film and video production and are deeply missed. Today's new crop of Native workers in the entertainment industry stand on the shoulders of these giants and owe much to these trailblazers.

CONTENTS

I began reading this book fearing it would be another look at the sorry history of the treatment of Native peoples in the film industry. Many of us who have spent a lifetime in this business are familiar with that history, with its inaccurate portrayals of our people along with misrepresentation of our cultures, our histories, and our tribal stories.

But that's not what this book is about. This is a book of true stories about Native people of different ages who have struggled and succeeded to create careers for themselves in the dog-eat-dog world that is the entertainment industry.

Thankfully, the author does give proper nods to those "ancestors" of film media work, such as Will Sampson, Gary Farmer, Bob Hicks, Chief Dan George, Mike Smith, and Phil Lucas. Their important contributions are well noted in these pages.

But I was most intrigued by stories of how a cadre of younger Native film and media artists are developing their special talents to offer as writers, technicians, actors, camera operators, and even producers and directors. How they all began working in film and media varies, from one who saw it as a lifelong goal to others who got some lucky breaks.

Each story should give a younger reader an insight into what it takes to work in the world of film—and it is a big world of opportunity. The biggest takeaway for readers is the honest advice given by these individuals, who found in themselves the talent, tenacity, self-esteem, work ethic, and very real desire to pursue their dream with a "never give up" attitude.

—FRANK BLYTHE

Eastern Band of Cherokee and Sisseton/Wahpeton Dakota

FOUNDING MEMBER AND EXECUTIVE DIRECTOR OF THE NATIVE AMERICAN PUBLIC BROADCASTING CONSORTIUM

In 2014, Vision Maker Media, formerly the Native American Public Broadcasting Consortium, created the Frank Blythe Media Excellence Award to honor Frank's lasting legacy for the advancement of Native American television programming and production. The award is presented each April during the Vision Maker Film Festival to recognize outstanding Native individuals who have made significant contributions in television, radio, and other forms of media.

Storytellers. That's what Native actors, writers, producers, directors, editors, and cinematographers are. They are modern-day storytellers who use the most advanced communication technologies possible to reach new and ever-widening audiences, combining traditional storytelling styles with twenty-first-century technology.

The act of storytelling is one of humanity's oldest pastimes, and Native Americans are among the best storytellers there have ever been. So why does it seem that Native people are mostly missing from movie, TV, and digital screens? Why have there been so relatively few nationally broadcast or distributed filmed Native stories starring Native actors, written and directed by Native writers and directors, and told from a Native point of view?

Answers to those questions can be found in the experiences and opinions of the Native trailblazers interviewed in this book, along with other questions such as these: How do you become a working actor or filmmaker? What obstacles have Native people faced in entertainment and production that members of other groups haven't? How has the entertainment industry changed with regard to Native American involvement in front of and behind the camera?

My own participation in entertainment and production began in the early 1980s, when I went to work in the communication department of the Muscogee-Creek Nation, located in Okmulgee, Oklahoma. It was my first job as a writer and video producer in Indian Country*, and it opened up a whole new world to me. I'd been raised as a city boy

---

*Indian Country is the term used to encompass the many self-governing Native American communities in the United States.

in Texas, the son of a radio station–announcer father and a fashion-model mother, far removed from our Native roots.

It was in the mid-1970s that my family's oral history revealed my Native heritage. I heard stories of ancestors who lived in an America in which Native Americans had little or no value, along with stories of previous generations who hid their identities in order to survive physically and socially.

The 1980s brought for me, among other things, interaction with Native actors such as Academy Award winner Wes Studi (Cherokee), playwright and stage director JR Mathews (Miami tribe), and Tulsa's active American Indian Theater Company of Oklahoma. National Indian communications conferences, held annually in that decade, introduced me to my future friend, mentor, and production partner, Phil Lucas, as well as to Blackfeet producer-director George Burdeau; Colville film-maker Glenn Raymond (1945–2010); Minneapolis filmmaker Chris Spotted Eagle (Houma); and American Indian Film Institute founder, Mike Smith (Fort Peck Sioux), just to name a few.

Frank Blythe, founding director of Native American Public Broadcasting Consortium, was an important part of the mix in those days. His prominent position and professional stature allowed him to bring Native filmmakers together and to support their early groundbreaking efforts to produce TV programming and be taken seriously within the industry.

Many other Native actors and filmmakers could have been included in these pages, but limits in time, space, scheduling, and other factors brought these twelve individuals into focus. Certainly, each and every Native person who has set foot in the entertainment arena, so to speak, has contributed something and left a mark in some way.

These contributions may have widened the path and opened a new direction for others to follow. As you'll read for yourself, many of the relative "newbies" in the field are very much aware of those who came before them.

Who knows? Maybe you'll become one of the Native actors or filmmakers who stand on the shoulders of trailblazers and tell the best Native stories ever told.

There are numerous Native people in the entertainment industry—too many to mention—and most of them unknown to the majority of people. Here is a list of just a few other Native actors and film-makers, living and deceased, that you could investigate online via wikipedia.org or imdb.com.

Gil Birmingham (Comanche): actor; *Yellowstone* and *Hell or High Water*

Gary Farmer (Indigenous Canadian): actor; *Powwow Highway*, *Dead Man*, and *The Red Road*

Hanay Geiogamah (Kiowa): theater professor, author, producer, playwright

Chief Dan George (1899–1981, Canadian/Coast Salish): actor; *Little Big Man* and *The Outlaw Josey Wales*

Rodney A. Grant (Omaha): actor; *Dances with Wolves* and *Hawkeye*

Saginaw Grant (Sac and Fox): actor; *Harts of the West* TV series and *Wind Walkers*

Graham Greene (Indigenous Canadian): actor; Academy Award nominee for Best Supporting Actor in *Dances with Wolves*

Sterlin Harjo (Seminole/Muscogee): director; *Barking Water* and *Mekko*

Bob Hicks (1934–2014, Muscogee-Creek): founder of First Americans in the Arts, filmmaker; *Return of the Country*

Swil Kanim/Richard Marshall (Lummi): actor, musician; *Northern Exposure* TV series and *The Business of Fancy Dancing*

Georgina Lightning (Cree/Canadian): producer; best known for *Older Than America*

Zahn McClarnon (Lakota): actor; *Longmire* and *Westworld*

Heather Rae (Cherokee descent): producer, director; *Trudell*, *Frozen River*, and *Wind Walkers*

Ricky Lee Regan (Muscogee-Creek): actor, director, graphic artist; *Ridiculous Six* and *Midnight Shanghai*

Will Sampson (1933–1987, Muscogee-Creek): actor; Academy Award nominee for Best Supporting Actor in *One Flew Over the Cuckoo's Nest*

Jay Silverheels (1912–1980, Mohawk): actor; *Lone Ranger* TV series

Wes Studi (Cherokee): actor; received an Academy Award in 2019 for his lifetime body of work

John Trudell (1946–2015, Lakota): actor, poet, activist; *Thunderheart* and *Smoke Signals*

Misty Upham (1982–2014, Blackfeet): actor; best known for *Frozen River* and the movie version of *August: Osage County*

Floyd Red Crow Westerman (1936–2007, Lakota): actor; *Dances with Wolves*

Irene Bedard

IÑUPIAT, YUP'IK, INUIT, CREE, MÉTIS ACTOR

For the general moviegoing public, Irene Bedard is most often thought of as the voice of Disney's Pocahontas. But her abilities, experience, and dedication to the craft of acting go far beyond this two-dimensional animated character.

At the age of eight, this actor of Iñupiat, Yup'ik, Inuit, Cree, and Métis heritage was already writing her own plays, and by age ten she was putting on those plays beneath the trees of her own backyard located in Anchorage, Alaska. Born in 1967 to Indigenous parents who were deeply involved in Alaska Native rights issues and struggles, Irene was unfortunately exposed at an early age to threats against her family from non-Native sources.

As a member of one of the few Native families in her school district, Irene recalls being chased home from the bus after school by kids with baseball bats. As the oldest child in her family, she felt a strong need to do something to keep other Native kids in the neighborhood safe. That's what led her to create small theater productions using her siblings as the actors, which kept them occupied and out of danger. Later, thanks to acting workshops and ballet classes, she performed with the Anchorage Community Theater and the Anchorage Civic Opera.

Irene began her college career with a scholarship to study physics and philosophy, but she shifted to drama when she transferred to the Ira Brind School of Theater Arts at the University of the Arts in Philadelphia. There she was trained by award-winning, internationally renowned dramatist and playwright Walter Dallas, who was honored as one of Philadelphia's one hundred history makers of the twentieth century.

During her final year of theater school, Irene traveled back and forth to one of the theatrical centers of the world, New York City, in order to establish a working base there. Operating out of the American Indian Community House, New York's urban Indian support organization, a Native group began writing and producing its own stage productions. One such project, *In the Spirit*, told the story of a group of young Native activists who were trying to make a difference in the world. The play was performed at several major New York City theaters.

After Irene moved to New York City full-time to pursue a career in acting, she met and started working with Randy Redroad, an aspiring Indigenous American film director. Like Randy, Irene held various day jobs to pay bills while auditioning for theater and film roles. During her lifetime, Irene has worked as a bartender, waitperson, librarian, and baker, just to name a few.

It is common for both experienced and inexperienced actors to maintain full-time or part-time jobs in other fields while simultaneously going after acting roles. This is due to the unpredictable nature of the acting profession, which often creates income gaps that actors have to fill by other means.

It was during her early days in New York that Irene found an agent, a crucial element of any successful acting career. "Ricki Olshan, at Don Buchwald & Associates, came to see one of my performances," Irene says. "At that time, no one else in Los Angeles or New York was seeking out Native talent, but this agent was. And she's still my agent to this day."

Soon after she acquired her agent, Irene received her first offer for a movie role—a three-picture deal with Warner Bros. and action actor Steven Seagal. Surprisingly, Irene turned down the deal because she felt the roles didn't portray the proper image for Native people or herself. Many people thought she was crazy to turn down a three-picture deal with Warner Bros. But it just didn't feel right for her, and her new agent supported that decision. This is the type of dilemma Native actors have to face all too often.

The next offer she received was for the role of Nakooma in the movie *Squanto: A Warrior's Tale*. The film is set in the early 1600s and is loosely based on the actual historical Native American figure of the same name who was captured and taken to England.

Later that same year, Irene was offered a more substantial role playing Mary Crow Dog in the Turner Network Television movie *Lakota Woman: Siege at Wounded Knee*. The film was based on actual events as depicted in Mary Crow Dog's autobiographical book of the same name. These events included the 1973 armed standoff between members of the American Indian Movement (AIM) and multiple law enforcement agencies on the Pine Ridge Indian Reservation in South Dakota. In real life in those days, AIM and other groups were protesting the way the US government had been treating Native American communities and individuals.

In 1995, Irene was nominated for the prestigious Golden Globe Award for Best Actress for that role, and the film was honored with the Western Heritage Award for Television Feature Film. Irene's acting work and award nomination catapulted her into the limelight, where she was noticed by Disney executives who were looking for a Native actress to provide the voice for Pocahontas in the animated movie the company was about to produce. Irene was still shooting *Lakota Woman* in South Dakota when she heard about the casting call for the new role.

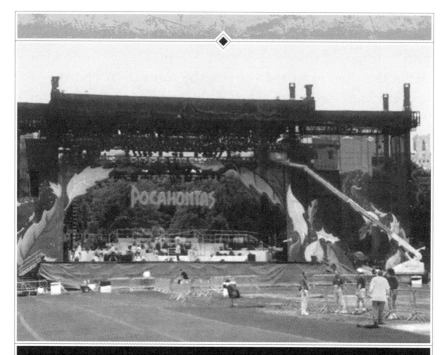

The premiere of Disney's *Pocahontas* was the largest in movie history, with about 100,000 people in attendance.

During a break in shooting, the young actress took a train to New York, where she auditioned for the part, and then immediately returned to the set of *Lakota Woman*. She was still finishing work on that film when she learned that she had gotten the job of voicing the Pocahontas animated character. A well-known Broadway actress-singer would provide the singing voice.

True to the Disney brand, company executives had already decided that *Pocahontas* the animated movie would be a romanticized, musical fairy-tale version of history. And those same movie executives made big plans to introduce the film to moviegoing families.

Their plans included the largest movie premiere in history, held in New York City's Central Park in June 1995. Approximately one hundred thousand people attended the screening, which utilized four eighty-foot screens and banks of huge sound speakers set up on the park's Great Lawn.

"I had a police motorcade that took me through the city from my house to the premiere in Central Park," Irene says of the event. "It was the largest movie premiere in history, but there had already been protests against the movie before it had even been released."

Film critics praised the film's animation, musical score, and songs, but criticized the story's lack of historical accuracy. Some Native American activists argued that the film presented and perpetuated damaging stereotypes of Native Americans while elevating the importance of the white colonists. On the other hand, AIM leader and actor Russell Means, who played the role of Pocahontas's father in the movie, defended the film, saying it was the "finest feature film on American Indians Hollywood has ever produced."

Irene, unfortunately, was thrust into the center of the controversy, and the media and the public expected her to speak out about the Native American image issues being discussed.

"I'm just a shy girl from Alaska," Irene remembers saying at the time. "I can't speak for all Native American people. No one can."

Thankfully, she had the full support of all her friends at the American Indian Community House, her family away from home, to help her face and deal with the pressure emotionally.

Lakota Woman: Siege at Wounded Knee had been one of five TV movies about Native American historical figures broadcast by Turner Network Television in the 1990s. Another was *Crazy Horse,* produced a couple of years later. Irene was cast as Black Buffalo Woman in that film, which portrayed the historical role Crazy Horse played in the Battle of the Little Bighorn.

Irene was able to really display her acting muscles in the 1996 HBO production of *Grand Avenue*, a contemporary tale about Native American survival in modern times. One of the executive producers of the film was Robert Redford, and the teleplay was written by Native author Greg Sarris. The story realistically depicts a brief period in the life of three related Native families living in Santa Rosa, California. One television critic called the production "television drama at its very best" and praised it for revealing "what life is like beyond the endless middle-class platitudes that dominate most prime-time programming."

The year 1998 brought a welcome breakthrough in Native American filmmaking with a low-budget independent movie written, directed, and acted by Native people. *Smoke Signals*, written by Sherman Alexie (Spokane/Coeur d'Alene) and directed by Chris Eyre (Cheyenne/Arapaho) was well received by mainstream critics and had a 98 percent rating on the website Rotten Tomatoes. The *Los Angeles Times* described *Smoke Signals* as a "warm film of friendship and reconciliation," while the *Austin Chronicle* newspaper stated, "The cast is uniformly excellent."

Irene played the character Suzy Song in the film, and *Rolling Stone* magazine called her portrayal "tough and luminous."

The late 1990s and early 2000s kept Irene busy with acting parts that included a *Pocahontas* sequel, multiple television series and movies, and other animated voice roles.

In 2004, Irene was picked to play the part of Margaret Light Shines Wheeler, a Native American character that appears in four episodes of the six-part TV miniseries *Into the West*. Executive produced by Steven Spielberg of Dreamworks Television, the historical series ran on Turner Network Television (TNT) in June and July 2005.

The plot follows the stories of two families—one white American, one Native American—from the 1820s to 1890. Their lives become intertwined through momentous events as American citizens move into and take over the American West. The large cast of the miniseries also included Native actors Gil Birmingham, Zahn McClarnon, Sheila Tousey, Russell Means, and Wes Studi, among many others.

Irene's list of more than sixty-four acting credits even includes the unique part of a future Native American president of the United States in hip-hop artist Jay-Z's 2018 music video *Family Feud*, featuring his wife, Beyoncé.

One of Irene's more recent projects is a TV series called *Radio Nowhere*, based on Stephen King's popular horror novel *The Stand*. The story is set in the future, when a deadly virus has killed much of the world's population. Irene isn't known for performing in horror films or even liking movies in that genre.

"Here I am doing *The Stand*, while my friends know that I can't even watch horror movies," she says. "But I've lived through what I call our 'Manifest Destiny characters' and the retelling of the horror of American history that way. I've had to relive for everyone, in story, the telling of the apocalypse of possibly one hundred million Indigenous people who lived on this island, Turtle Island. So, in a way, I've been doing horror my whole career."

Another common thread she finds in some of the characters she plays is that of protector. In the TV series *The Mist* (2017), her character, Kimi Lucero, is a protector of the elderly women in the story. In *Radio Nowhere*, her character also protects another important character in that story.

What advice would Irene offer young Native people considering creative careers? "We're such creative people culturally. Storytelling seems to come naturally to our people. Whether we're into graphic novels or writing or acting, everything we do comes out of beauty," she says.

One final point Irene likes to make when talking to young people is this: "You are the only you to exist from the beginning of time to the end of time. You're that unique. You may not feel particularly special right now, but you are able to re-create yourself. Like the caterpillar that transforms into a butterfly, you can re-create yourself into something incredibly beautiful. Each of us has some hidden superpower. You have to look deep to find yours and bring it out."

SELECTED FILMOGRAPHY (ACTING)

2020: *FBI: Most Wanted* (TV series); Marilou Skye

2019: *Heartland* (feature film); Mary Singing Crow

2018: *Westworld* (TV series); Wichapi

2018: *Ralph Breaks the Internet* (animated feature); Pocahontas (voice)

2017: *The Mist* (TV series); Kimi Lucero

2012–2015: *Longmire* (TV series); May Stillwater

2008–2009: *The Spectacular Spider-Man* (animated TV series); Jean DeWolff (voice)

2005: *Into the West* (TV miniseries); Margaret Light Shines Wheeler

2000: *Roughnecks: The Starship Troopers Chronicles* (TV series); Gen. Miriam Redwing

1998: *Smoke Signals* (feature film); Suzy Song

1998: *Naturally Native* (feature film); Tanya Lewis

1995: *Pocahontas* (animated feature film); Pocahontas (speaking voice)

1994: *Squanto: A Warrior's Tale* (feature film); Nakooma

1994: *Lakota Woman: Siege at Wounded Knee* (TV movie); Mary Crow Dog

Tantoo Cardinal

MÉTIS, CREE, DENE, NAKOTA ACTOR

With more than one hundred and twenty acting credits to her name, Tantoo Cardinal is one of the longest working and most recognizable Native actors on the North American continent. Born in 1950 in northern Alberta, Canada, she is of Métis, Cree, Dene, and Nakota ancestry.

She was raised by her grandmother in the small, isolated town of Fort McMurray with little connection to the outside world. Everyone in that tight-knit community looked out for one another, she says, and the first school she attended was a one-room schoolhouse.

When it came time for Tantoo to attend high school, Ted Walker, a junior high teacher, got her enrolled in a school in Edmonton, the capital of the province of Alberta. Arrangements were made for Tantoo to stay with a Mennonite family there. Several families in that community allowed students to stay with them while they were attending school.

During that time, Tantoo met Fred Martin, an American Mennonite pacifist who had fled to Canada to escape the military draft. At that time, the United States was sending young American men to fight the war in Vietnam. Fred had been active in the civil rights movement, working with Dr. Martin Luther King Jr. to organize protests and marches in Alabama.

Through her interactions with Fred, Tantoo came to understand that she was a survivor of the attempted genocide of generations of her people, perpetrated by the European immigrants who settled and colonized Canada.

"Our Native cultures were outlawed," she explains. "I came along around the time my generation was hauling our culture back out of the darkness and the unlawful state in which it had been placed."

Tantoo was becoming more aware of the social changes occurring then and decided to volunteer for causes that were helping improve the lives of Native peoples. She wanted to find a way to make a significant contribution to these efforts.

"Acting was just one of the things I did at that time when I was exploring ways to make a difference," she says. "Changing minds and hearts, I guess, by telling the truth of our Indigenous history, because so many lies had been told about us."

Her first acting opportunities came through the Native Communications Society, directed by Jeff Howard, in Edmonton. Jeff was creating short films, ten to thirty minutes long, for various agencies, including the Department of Indian Affairs, Department of Manpower, and others. One of those projects was *He Comes without Calling*, a thirty-three-minute piece completed in 1975.

The film, addressed to Indigenous Canadian families, warned of the dangers of fire in the home. The story features a ghostly visitor who comes in the night to identify fire hazards in the family's home. Also performing in the film was Chief Dan George, who had already played Old Lodge Skins in the 1970 hit movie *Little Big Man*, a part that got him nominated for an Oscar for Best Actor in a Supporting Role.

Later, in the 1980s, Tantoo was cast in the Canadian TV series *Spirit Bay*, which ran for three years. Some said this was an inspirational series that paved the way for future First Nations and Indigenous Canadian television programming. Viewers commented that *Spirit Bay* provided a realistic look at the lives of Ojibway people on a northern Ontario reserve.

ABC's *Stumptown* stars Tantoo Cardinal as Sue Lynn Blackbird.

Another of her early acting gigs was in the 1987 feature film *Loyalties*, the story of a pedophile medical doctor who comes to a small community, fleeing the city where he was accused of child molestation. This movie project helped bring this issue into public awareness.

Tantoo's performance in that film was called "stirring," and she received a Genie Award nomination from the Academy of Canadian Cinema & Television. For that role, she won the Best Actress Award at the American Indian Film Festival in San Francisco, the People's Choice Award at the Toronto Film Festival, and other international awards.

The next big project came in just a couple of years when Tantoo played a character named Black Shawl in the global hit movie *Dances with Wolves* starring Kevin Costner. At the time, the film was considered a major breakthrough in terms of its authentic portrayal of Native Americans, as close attention was paid to tribal language, clothing, culture, and lifeways. Even though some Native individuals criticized the film because it was written and directed by non-Natives, Tantoo believes it did a lot of good for Native people overall.

"That movie opened some doors," Tantoo says. "It encouraged more of our people to get involved in the industry and also showed that there are Native people who can act and perform other entertainment industry jobs."

During the production of that film, as well as others, Tantoo spoke up when she felt her character was being asked to talk or behave in ways that were not accurate representations of tribal people. She admits that there are good ways to do this and not-so-good ways. She says that as an actor, you have to respect those who "hold the purse strings," meaning the people who have the power to hire or fire you. You can ask for changes in the script or to the direction, but if the answer is no, you have to accept it and move on.

Tantoo received top billing as the female lead in the 1993 movie *Where the Rivers Flow North*, playing a Native character named Bangor. The film, called an "overlooked gem" by one critic, revolves around a man and his wife whose lands are threatened by the impending construction of a dam. Several reviewers wrote that Tantoo's performance was Oscar-worthy, though neither she nor the film were nominated.

Tantoo worked fairly steadily through the decade of the '90s, appearing in several episodes of a US television series set in the 1800s, *Dr. Quinn, Medicine Woman*, and several episodes of the very popular Canadian series *North of 60*, which takes place in a contemporary Canadian Indigenous community.

A film that marked another major breakthrough in Native involvement in the entertainment industry was 1998's *Smoke Signals*, written by Native author Sherman Alexie and directed by Cheyenne filmmaker Chris Eyre. The mostly Native cast included Tantoo, who played Arlene Joseph, the mother of one of the main characters.

One reviewer called the film "the best film ever made that captures real characters and the spirit of modern Native Americans." Another wrote, "It was shocking to realize that as late as 1998, this was still one of the few movies made by insiders, written, directed, and acted by Native Americans."

As time moved into the twenty-first century, the busy actor continued to command the screen and garner significant acting accomplishments in both film and television projects. These included the 2003 two-night miniseries *Dreamkeeper*, which recounted the life-changing journey of an angry Lakota young man and his grandfather, and the 2008 *Older Than America* feature film that exposed abuses in Native American boarding schools.

In recent years, Tantoo has been highly sought after for film and TV projects, so she has been busier than at almost any other time in her life. Her acting credits include nine projects in 2018 and approximately the same number in 2019.

She played the role of Grandmother Ruth in the 2019 feature film *Red Snow*, which is the story of an Indigenous Canadian soldier who is captured by the Taliban and finds himself reflecting on the death of his cousin back home. The film, written and directed by Métis filmmaker Marie Clements, was made possible with the support of several Canadian agencies, including the CBC Breaking Barriers Feature Film Fund, Telefilm Canada, the Women in the Director's Chair Feature Film Award, the Canada Media Fund, Aboriginal Peoples Television Network, and several others.

"I'm interested to see how audiences will take this movie," Tantoo says. "It's a view into cultural commonality between tribal communities separated by thousands of miles."

Tantoo and the director were both present at the LA Skins Fest in November 2019, when the film was given the Best Achievement in Film award.

Also in 2019, *Stumptown,* a new dramatic television series about a female private investigator, received significant positive attention in the media and among Tantoo's supporters. The series, set in Portland, Oregon, features a recurring Native character, Sue Lynn Blackbird, the tough-minded chairperson of her tribe. Broadcast in prime time on the ABC network, the series is based on a popular graphic novel of the same name.

"A part like this has been a long time coming," Tantoo says. "Sue Lynn is the kind of strong Native female character that cuts through the stereotypes and shows one of the ways a modern woman of integrity and vision can lead her tribe."

When addressing young people who might be thinking about getting into the entertainment industry, Tantoo has quite a bit of sound advice.

"If you're getting involved to be famous or rich, there are only a few people who manage that," she cautions. "You really have to love what you're doing and have a sense of purpose in order just to stay with it because it's so hard to get noticed and find work. However, if you feel you are placed here in this life for that purpose, then stay with it, whatever it takes."

She feels that most Indigenous people in North America are "coming back from genocide," to use her phrase. An examination of Native history shows that European settlers were intent on wiping out the Indigenous people of the Americas. That's what many Native people are working through and attempting to go beyond, even today.

"When you find your path in life, expect it to be difficult," Tantoo says. "But expect it to be rewarding as well, because there's something about releasing a darkness and finding your truth that's very fulfilling. Your understanding of the truth will change as you go along and become more experienced, and then you'll start to see things more expansively."

During her accomplished career, Tantoo has received many awards and honors for her work both on- and off-screen. She is a member of the Order of Canada, one of that nation's highest civilian honors. The Order recognized the actor for her contributions to the growth and development of Indigenous performing arts.

In 2015, Tantoo was honored with the ACTRA (Alliance of Canadian Cinema, Television and Radio Artists) Award of Excellence. Tantoo's other honors include: the Sterling Award in Theater for *All My Relations*, the Totem Award given by the First Americans in the Arts organization in Los Angeles, American Indian Film Festival's Best Actress Award, a Gemini Award for *North of 60*, and a Leo Award for her part in the series *Blackstone*. The impressive list goes on and on. There seems to be no end in sight for this dedicated, stronghearted woman.

SELECTED FILMOGRAPHY

2019–2020: *Stumptown* (TV series); Sue Lynn Blackbird

2019: *See* (TV series); The Dreamer

2019: *Red Snow* (feature film); Grandmother Ruth

2018: *Falls Around Her* (feature film); Mary Birchbark

2017: *Wind River* (feature film); Alice Crowheart

2017: *Godless* (TV miniseries); Iyovi

2015–2017: *Longmire* (TV series); Crow Medicine Woman

2012: *Blackstone* (TV series); Wilma Stoney

2011: *Shouting Secrets* (feature film); June

2008: *Older Than America* (feature film); Auntie Apple

2003–2006: *Moccasin Flats* (TV series); Betty Merasty

2003: *Dreamkeeper* (TV movie); Old Pawnee woman

2000: *Navigating the Heart* (TV movie); Mary

1998: *Smoke Signals* (feature film); Arlene Joseph

1996: *Grand Avenue* (TV movie); Nellie

1994: *Lakota Woman: Siege at Wounded Knee* (TV movie); Mary's mother

1993–1995: *Dr. Quinn, Medicine Woman* (TV series); Snow Bird

1993: *Where the Rivers Flow North* (feature film); Bangor

1991: *Black Robe* (feature film); Chomina's wife

1990: *Dances with Wolves* (feature film); Black Shawl

1988: *War Party* (feature film); Sonny's mother

1987: *Loyalties* (feature film); Rosanne Ladouceur

1984: *Spirit Bay* (TV series); Annie

1975: *He Comes without Calling* (short film)

Christopher Nataanii Cegielski

DINÉ (NAVAJO) WRITER, PRODUCER, DIRECTOR

Christopher Nataanii Cegielski is a filmmaker of Diné (Navajo), Polish, French, and Irish descent. Born in Los Angeles in 1991, he mostly grew up in Flagstaff, Arizona. With older siblings off at school each day, he spent a lot time on his own or with friends playing outside. His house was across the road from one of the largest ponderosa pine forests in the United States, and that basically served as his playground and arena of exploration.

He remembers spending many days "messing around, getting into trouble, and finding adventure." With active imaginations, he and his friends created stories and played characters within those stories, improvised changes,

Christopher Nataanii Cegielski.

and revised the outcome as a story progressed. Each new day brought a fresh imaginative scenario to play out.

"I think my generation was the last group of kids that could grow up without a device in their hands," he says. "We didn't grow up looking at screens and being informed by other peoples' experiences. We went out into the world and interacted with it firsthand rather than through other people's expressions shared on social media."

For the most part, Christopher's young life was spent away from Navajo culture, with only occasional visits to his grandmother and other relatives on the reservation, even though his home was close by. It wasn't until his high school and college years that he became interested and more curious about that aspect of his background.

It was in high school that he started wanting to become a writer. He felt that he had a knack for storytelling, and writing was the most immediate way to express himself. In college he did a lot of creative writing but began to feel the need to incorporate visual expressions like those one would see in a film.

After some research, Christopher found that the University of Arizona in Tucson had a film/TV production program as well as a bachelor of fine arts (BFA) degree program. Once students got into the BFA program, they would have the chance to make a film. That's where he made his first short film, *Bloodlines*, in the year 2014. It's the story of two brothers who seek to earn their father's respect by hunting the wolf that's been killing their livestock.

During the time he was writing that filmscript and directing it, Christopher was also trying to figure out who he was and what he wanted to do with his life. He was questioning the lifestyle patterns that were expected of him by his family. Would he finish college, get his degree, find a job, earn a decent amount of money, get married, have kids, and so forth? Or would he find his dream and follow it, no matter where that led? All those questions came into his mind as he was working on that film.

In addition to those issues, he had to make his small production budget of two thousand dollars go as far as it could, which meant that most people who worked on the film didn't get paid. Instead, they donated their time and expertise. So Christopher had to work around their schedules and shoot certain scenes when his volunteer actors and crew were available.

"If you've got a lot of money to pay people, obviously you can tell them what to do, when to do it, and how to do it," he explains. "But when you have a small amount of funds, you're asking people for a lot of favors, and you have to work around people's timelines. It's harder to get the film done and it takes longer, but getting it done right pays off in the end."

He knew that if he took his time in creating this film, it could help him get noticed as a film director. In turn, that could lead to opportunities to direct other films with larger budgets.

After graduating from the university, Christopher moved back to Flagstaff to help his father and think about his future. He had entered *Bloodlines* into Canada's imagineNATIVE Film + Media Arts Festival but didn't know if it would be accepted. He was soon delighted to learn that not only did the festival accept his film but they also offered to pay for his flight and hotel expenses if he wanted to attend the event. Of course, he said yes.

Since this would be his first film festival, Christopher wanted to find out what these events are all about. He researched what goes on at film festivals and interacted with other Native filmmakers. They offered him advice on how to conduct himself professionally, how to mingle and network with others from the filmmaking industry, and how to make the most of this opportunity.

Attending the festival opened his eyes to the possibilities of being a professional filmmaker. He got to meet television executives who buy television programming, producers and directors looking for scripts, and financiers who invest in movie projects. He met with programmers from the Sundance

Cast and crew of Christopher's "Grandma Running" commercial for New Balance shoes.

Film Festival and the Berlin International Film Festival in Germany. He found the whole weeklong event inspiring and energizing.

"I also met several Native filmmakers who showed me that if I believe in what I'm doing, if I believe in creating filmed stories, I could actually do this for a living," Christopher says. "I realized this wasn't as crazy a career path as I first thought."

When he got back home to Flagstaff, Christopher decided it was time to move to Los Angeles. He packed up a few things and headed west, but on his way to LA, he got a message from the Berlin International Film Festival in Germany. They asked him to submit *Bloodlines* to their festival, and this got Christopher very excited.

His *Bloodlines* short film was screened at a total of fourteen festivals over the next couple of years. The young man felt very fortunate that his film was accepted to these venues.

On top of that, the Sundance Institute's Native American Producers Lab invited him to submit an application, and he was accepted into that program in 2015. During that session, he completed the script for his next short film, *Movement through the Valley*, a supernatural story about two Navajo cops investigating a series of murders on the rez.

At the Sundance lab, Christopher was encouraged to expand the project into a feature film script. So after completing the short script, he worked on expanding it into a feature. Because the twenty-two-year-old was so excited about turning the project into something bigger, he didn't take the time to ask himself whether it was the right thing for him to do.

"At a young age, I felt like I needed to take every opportunity that was given to me," he recounts. "So I worked and reworked that script, but no matter how hard I worked on it, it was turning out to be this movie that was a combination of the two TV shows *The X-Files* and *Law & Order*."

A year and a half later, he decided it wouldn't be a good first feature film to have his name on. He went back to his *Bloodlines* story and worked on an expanded version of that script, but he added a supernatural aspect to it.

On a separate track, a Los Angeles–based organization named Film Independent offered Christopher a chance to take part in something they called Project Involve. This project takes filmmakers from underrepresented communities and provides them with the resources to direct a short film while also allowing them to network with other filmmakers.

Through Project Involve, Christopher created *Reagan*, a short film written and produced by other participants in the program. This allowed him to see what it was like to direct a film that other people wrote and produced, something he would no doubt be asked to do in his future career. He learned some big lessons on that project, the most important one being that he had no business directing that film. The story was about a young girl growing up in foster homes in San Francisco who ends up living on the streets. He really knew nothing of the character's life experiences, and he realized while editing the film that he wasn't doing justice to the subject matter.

"Some directors, obviously, direct stories with elements they've never lived through," he explains. "But they have substitute experiences in their lives that allow them to understand the emotions these characters are going through. I didn't have that in this case."

After his experience with *Reagan*, Christopher decided to find a cowriter to work with him on the feature film version of his *Bloodlines* script. This became a sort of background project that the pair worked on in their spare time. Meanwhile, Christopher worked at whatever jobs he could find to pay his monthly bills.

One of the jobs he had, starting in the summer of 2016, was teaching video-production workshops to Native youth on the Navajo reservation. This project, funded through a grant secured by Paper Rocket Productions in Flagstaff, paid leaders to run these workshops in remote areas of the reservation that were prone to drug abuse and suicide.

The following summer, Christopher taught a similar workshop on the Pine Ridge reservation in South Dakota through a different organization, Outlast Film Camp. That organization's goal is to give youth from minority communities the tools to depict stories that share their view of the world.

"These media workshops are about more than just making videos," Christopher says. "I realize that most of these kids aren't going to become filmmakers, but the process gets them thinking about what they might want to say and how to say it. It teaches them about planning and teamwork, and it teaches them about directing a group of people to strive for the same goal. Those are good skills to have in lots of situations."

Another opportunity that came Christopher's way was a Sony Pictures Diversity Fellowship, which was awarded to him when he finished his work with Project Involve. It

Christopher with his two lead actors, Colleen Biakeddy and Micah Chee on the "Grandma Running" production.

included a grant for ten thousand dollars, which he could use for any purpose, from paying rent to funding his own short film.

That grant got him thinking about what he really wanted to do at this point in his life. One thing he'd been interested in for a long time was directing TV ads. He learned that a good way to get started is to create what are called "spec commercials," which demonstrate how you would direct a TV commercial for a real or imaginary product. The objective is to showcase your approach to a particular subject, along with your skills and abilities.

Using the funds from the Sony Pictures Diversity Fellowship, he created three spec spots (another term for commercials) for Wings of America, a nonprofit Native American organization that promotes healthy lifestyles through running. When the commercials were completed, Christopher offered them to the organization, which greatly appreciated them.

The young filmmaker was confident that these spots would secure him work as a commercial director, but when he showed them to a production company, they asked, "What else do you have?"

He told them these were all he had, and they explained that he needed to have five or six examples of spec commercials for five or six different clients. His spots were all for one client and therefore only counted as one commercial. That was a disappointing blow, but Christopher got busy trying to raise money to make more specs.

He contacted Bird Runningwater at the Sundance Institute again to see if he knew of any other programs or opportunities he could apply to, particularly for commercials. Bird told him about the Commercial Directors Diversity Program (CDDP).

Christopher investigated the program and was delighted to find that, in addition to going to workshops and meeting

Christopher working with lead actor Colleen Biakeddy during production of the "Grandma Running" commercial.

people in that part of the business, the program supplied participants with fifteen thousand dollars to produce a spec commercial.

"So, for the first time in a while, I didn't have to use my own money to make another project," he said. "That was extremely awesome."

He sent in an application, submitted sample work, and was accepted into the program. Once the program started, he thought really hard about what kind of commercial he wanted to create. He knew it had to be unlike anything he had done before while still including something from his own Native culture.

In a conversation with his mother and sister, Christopher remembered seeing an elderly Diné (Navajo) woman herding her sheep in Canyon de Chelly on the reservation. She was very agile and mobile as she guided her animals down a rock-filled hillside.

He also remembered regularly seeing elder Diné women at powwows and other Native events wearing their traditional clothing. But instead of moccasins, they always wore Nike or Adidas running shoes. That struck him as a humorous and interesting juxtaposition—the traditional and the new mixed together.

This got his imagination going as he merged the sheep-herding scenario with the idea that these elderly "superwomen" had to be ready at a moment's notice for some unexpected emergency.

"We often have these outside filmmakers who know nothing about our culture coming in and highlighting the poverty or alcoholism or other negatives," Christopher explains. "I wanted to send the narrative in a new direction and show something that was more positive, especially for Native youth."

When it came time to pitch his spec commercial idea, Christopher told the CDDP people about his "Grandma Running" concept. The setting is a rocky canyon on the Navajo reservation where a sheepherding family lives. One day a young boy in the family discovers that one of their sheep has escaped, so he yells, "Grandma, sheep running away!" That's when his grandma, dressed in her New Balance running shoes, shifts into action. Performing daring jumps and flips through the rocky landscape, with plenty of close-ups of her shoes, the elder finds and captures the escapee, returning it safely to the corral.

Reverie Productions, the Los Angeles–based company that assisted with the production of the commercial, loved the idea. With their help, Christopher put together a team and found a location near the community of Pinon, Arizona, on the reservation. A very good casting director, who had cast other projects on the Navajo reservation, went to work finding the actress to play the spot's grandma. They shot the commercial over two hot days in August 2019, and Christopher was very pleased with the results.

"Even though people said it was impossible for me to become a filmmaker, I never really listened to them," he says. "There are people who are going to be movie directors, people who will become actors, and people who become doctors, lawyers, etc. Why couldn't I become a director? I knew what I felt inside my heart, and I chose to bet on myself."

SELECTED FILMOGRAPHY

2019: *For Any Run* (spec commercial); director

2018: *Heroines* (short film); producer

2017: *Scrimmage* (short film); second assistant director

2016: *Reagan* (short film); director

2015: *Wings of America Mentorship Camp* (short documentary); camera operator, editor

2015: *Bloodlines*; writer, director

2014: *Wings of America Mentorship Camp* (short film); camera operator, editor

Note to readers: You can view Christopher's wonderful spec commercial online at youtube.com/watch?v=DZuU95E8UTU.

Sydney Freeland

DINÉ (NAVAJO) WRITER, DIRECTOR

Sydney Freeland is a transgender Diné (Navajo) filmmaker who has had an impressive career so far. Born in 1980 in Gallup, New Mexico, she attended elementary and middle school there. Her high school years were spent in Farmington, New Mexico, at Navajo Preparatory School, a school designed to help get more Navajo students ready for college.

Growing up, she was active in sports, particularly cross-country track. She continued her education after high school, first at Arizona State University in Tempe, Arizona, where she made the track-and-field team. After three years, Sydney was cut from the team and had to find another subject to major in.

She began studying the field of fine art, taking classes in drawing, painting, and finally computer animation. In her final semester at Arizona State, she took a class in video produc-

Sydney Freeland.

Sydney describing a camera shot for an episode of a TV series.

tion. This introduced her to a brand-new option: the possibility of filmmaking as a career. She says that when she was growing up on the reservation, the concept of making films as a job didn't exist.

"There were a lot of artists in my family on the reservation," Sydney says. "They were involved in traditional mediums like weaving, jewelry making, pottery, and painting. I was surrounded by artists growing up, but no one was talking about filmmaking or animation."

So she did a Google search to try to find a graduate program to learn filmmaking. The first school in the alphabetized list of results was the Academy of Art University (AAU) in San Francisco. That sounded perfect to her, so she applied and was accepted. Two and a half years later, she graduated from the program with a master of fine arts degree in film.

She immediately moved to Los Angeles, the place where most of the country's television and movie productions, as well as production companies, are headquartered.

"I, of course, started at the bottom with a job that's called production assistant, or PA," she explains. "Basically, you're a grunt. You do all the odd jobs and run errands, the tasks that no one else wants to do."

On the job, she learned all she could about the production process, finally working her way into assisting in both the camera and editing departments. Working steadily, she stepped into camera operating, assistant editing, and then ultimately editing. Between these crew gigs, she began writing a script that eventually became her first feature film.

During this time, Sydney had to make a lot of sacrifices in order to get work and prove herself. The PA jobs don't pay very much, but it's where you have to start.

"You have to really want this, because I had to sleep on friends' couches," she says. "It means accepting a lot of rejection, a lot of not getting the job you're going after. I got just enough acceptance and work to keep me going."

Sydney thinks that film and television production work can be easily compared to working construction. In both jobs you work on a project intensely for a set number of hours or days or weeks, and then the job is over. When you're done with that one, you have to go out and find the next job. That process defined her life for several years.

Her first breakthrough came in 2009, when she was accepted into Sundance Institute's Native Filmmakers Lab. There she received critical assistance in writing her first feature script, *Drunktown's Finest*. The title refers to the unflattering nickname for her hometown.

The following year, Sydney was able to participate in Sundance Institute's Feature Film Screenwriters Lab, the Directors Lab, Music Composers Lab, and finally the Producers Summit. Each of these intense labs provides emerging filmmakers with access to talented, experienced producers, directors, or music composers who offer feedback on their specific projects.

During the Directors Lab, she had the chance to direct four scenes from her *Drunktown's Finest* screenplay with guidance and feedback from established filmmakers.

The Music Composers Lab paired Sydney with an experienced movie music composer who explained all the steps required to match music to a film and create original music for a feature film project. The music coordinator for a movie obtains the rights to use existing music and often hires the composer. A movie's music editor puts pieces of music in the film so the music is supporting and enhancing what's happening on-screen.

The final stage in Sydney's Sundance Institute experience was the Producers Summit, where she learned, among other things, how to use crowdfunding sites, such as GoFundMe and Kickstarter, to help raise money for a project. She was also introduced to the Netflix streaming service and learned about that company's growing role in distributing TV programs and movies to audiences all over the world.

When it finally came time for Sydney to actually produce her movie, Sundance Institute's founder, Robert Redford, signed on as the film's executive producer. This very positive development added credibility to the film, which helped investors feel confident about investing money in the production. But in spite of all the positive input and development that went into the movie, many investors were still reluctant to invest money in it.

"The most common response was, 'There's no audience for that,'" Sydney recalls. "They believed no one would want to see a movie about the contemporary struggles of young Native Americans."

However, Sydney persevered, completed the film on a minimal budget, and entered it in the Sundance Film Festival, where it was shown in 2014. According to Sydney, there are many benefits to having your film premiere at Sundance. "For one thing, your work is exposed to entertainment industry executives who wouldn't otherwise see it. And you also have an encouraging support system around you from the Sundance staff itself."

That Sundance screening inspired Sydney to first get a manager, then an agent, and finally an entertainment lawyer. That team, in turn, helped even more people in the industry become familiar with Sydney's work and experience. The bottom line is that they helped elevate her status and get more work for her.

"These three people are like part of your sales team," she says. "They help 'sell' you to producers and people in the industry who are looking to hire certain types of filmmakers to do specific jobs on upcoming productions." Sydney explains that your agent and manager can send out your resume and set up meetings with studio executives and producers. Then, if one of them offers you a job, your attorney can review the contract before you sign it to make sure it is a good deal for you.

"A good agent, manager, and attorney can handle the business side of things," Sydney says. "That leaves you to focus on the creative side, the fun side of the work."

Of course, you have to pay a percentage of your income to those people—the manager, agent, and attorney—for doing those jobs on your behalf. But you'll have more work and therefore more income from which to pay them.

Another outcome from premiering *Drunktown's Finest* at the Sundance Film Festival were invitations to show the film at other film festivals. Within the first couple of years, the film showed at sixteen festivals. Since then, it has been featured at more than one hundred festivals around the world, including LGBTQ festivals, Native American festivals, and other independent film festivals. That provides a lot of opportunities for a film's director to travel, get great publicity, and meet wonderful people.

An additional reason for showing a film at festivals is to get a distributor, which is a company that can get your movie

Sydney working with actors on a TV series.

into theaters and other screening outlets. After about a year of film-festival showings, Sydney found a distributor that got the film into a few theaters. But it was a disappointing result.

So she and the film's producer decided to self-distribute their movie, which meant they had to contact movie theater owners directly. They started with theaters located in the Southwest region, the area where the movie was made. Their first opportunity came from a theater in Santa Fe, New Mexico, that agreed to show it one weekend. The theater owner said that if it did well enough, he'd run it a second weekend. It ended up showing there for five weeks.

Then a theater chain in Arizona agreed to show it in Phoenix and Flagstaff under the same conditions. As long as the film made a certain amount of money, the theaters would continue to show it. *Drunktown's Finest* ran for six weeks in both theaters.

While this was going on, Sydney traveled to film festivals to show the film and was also trying to find production jobs. On top of that, she began writing what she hoped would become her second movie.

In the midst of these activities, her manager sent her a filmscript for which the writer was seeking a director. The script was called *Deidra & Laney Rob a Train*, the story of two sisters who live in a trailer park and decide to rob a train to get the money they need to bail their mother out of jail.

Sydney met with the writer and they hit it off. Sydney had never directed a project she hadn't written, so she was a little nervous about it. But, together, the director and the writer started pitching the project to producers.

In the meantime, a pair of writers approached Sydney in Los Angeles to see whether she would be interested in directing a TV/web series they'd written. Called *Her Story*, the series looked into the dating lives of transgender and gay women who were coming to terms with their sexual identity. The good news was that the series already had funding.

"That was a blessing that sort of fell out of the sky while all this other stuff was going on in the background," Sydney explains. "It moved forward really quickly. We met in January, and by April we were shooting."

After *Her Story* was completed and premiered online, Sydney turned her attention back to *Deidra & Laney Rob a Train*. They (the writer and the director) first pitched it to a pair of producers who seemed to be a good fit for the project. Then all four of them pitched the film to Netflix.

For that pitch, Sydney created a "lookbook," which provides a visual presentation (photographs, drawings, slides, multimedia) that help convey the look, tone, and feel of the movie. Creating a lookbook for a proposed project is something Sydney learned to do in film school.

Based on that pitch meeting, the Netflix streaming service bought the project. The director was surprised and pleased. What a contrast with trying to get *Drunktown's Finest* financed and made! This time, Netflix simply wrote them a check and said, "Here—now go and shoot it."

The team shot *Diedra & Laney Rob a Train* in 2016 and edited it in the fall. It premiered at Sundance in January 2017.

Netflix started showing the film soon afterward, and it provided a good example of Sydney's work, as she was becoming more interested in episodic television production (TV series).

Sydney's agent and manager got busy setting up meetings with TV producers and showrunners, the people who have creative control and management responsibility for television series programs. In the TV series production business, a different director is hired for each episode, although all the other positions keep the same personnel from episode to episode. The look and tone of the series are set by the showrunner, so the new directors are expected to do their job within an already established framework.

That's a far cry from directing a movie, for which the director has the final say on all creative decisions, including casting, locations, set design, wardrobe, hairstyles, actor makeup, and so forth. Then, after the shooting is complete, the director is immediately immersed in editing for several weeks. This includes making decisions about music and sound editing, image color corrections, and visual effects.

"The difference between directing episodic television and directing movies is that with episodic TV you're only involved with one segment of the process," Sydney says. "With a typical one-hour show, I'll have about eight days of preparation. The show has already been cast, locations selected, sets built—the whole thing is already in progress. After that, I'll have eight days to shoot the episode and about four days to edit. Then I'm all done and ready to move on."

After the TV director has finished her part, the showrunner may come in and make some minor editing changes. That's followed by a review by people from the network that will be airing the show. If anyone doesn't like how a scene turned out or if the scene just doesn't work, they will ask to have that part redone and shot again. The director would then have to schedule time to come back to the studio and direct the reshoot.

The very first TV episode Sydney was hired for was a brand-new series on Paramount Network called *Heathers*.

Sydney checks a camera shot during production of a TV series.

The next opportunity was for the long-running series *Grey's Anatomy*. From that point on, she's been able to work on many different TV series.

As a Native American transgender person, Sydney most enjoys opportunities to work on projects that have Native American or transgender/LGBTQ themes and characters. She says that the TV production business moves so fast that you don't usually have a chance to get to know much about the people you're working with. And most of the time, the people who hire you don't care what your background is as long as you can do the work efficiently.

One experience that stands out for Sydney was on a show she directed in 2019 called *Tales of the City*. This series airs on Netflix, and the particular episode she was hired to direct, "Rainbow Warriors," features a transgender actress named Daniela Vega. The actress had appeared in a movie made in Chile that won the Academy Award for Best Foreign Language Film the previous year. Because Daniela and Sydney had the shared experience of being transgender, they felt very comfortable working together, and that interaction made the project more meaningful to both of them.

Looking back at her life and career so far, Sydney feels she's come a long way. Going from a young person living on the reservation, who didn't even know that filmmaking was a paying job, to now being in the middle of directing television productions on a daily basis is a huge leap.

"Every shoot I've done has been a learning experience," she says. "Every production has its own challenges. I think the one constant in this business is that there is no constant."

SELECTED FILMOGRAPHY

2020: *Nancy Drew* (TV series, 1 episode)

2019: *Tales of the City* (TV series, 1 episode)

2019: *Impulse* (TV series, 1 episode)

2019: *Fear the Walking Dead* (TV series, 1 episode)

2018: *Heathers* (TV series, 1 episode)

2018: *Grey's Anatomy* (TV series, 1 episode)

2017: *Deirdra & Laney Rob a Train* (feature film)

2016: *Her Story* (web series)

2014: *Drunktown's Finest* (feature film)

2012: *Hoverboard* (short film)

CHAPTER 5

Kimberly Norris Guerrero

COLVILLE ACTOR, WRITER, PRODUCER, EDUCATOR

K imberly Guerrero is a multifaceted talent who is often recognized as Jerry Seinfeld's Native American girlfriend in a 1993 episode of the *Seinfeld* comedy television series. Not only is she an actor on stage and screen but she is also a writer, producer, and educator. An enrolled member of the Colville Confederated Tribes, she also carries Salish-Kootenai and Cherokee ancestry.

Her birthplace was Muskogee, Oklahoma, but she was raised in Idabel, a small rural community located in the southeast corner of the state. Her teenage mother was unprepared

Kimberly Norris Guerrero.

for raising a child and gave her up as a baby. A kind Anglo family with the last name of Norris adopted and raised her. Kimberly felt loved and accepted by her adoptive family and bears no ill feelings toward her biological mother.

Luckily, her new parents were sensitive to their daughter's need to grow up with access to some aspect of Native culture, so they gave her opportunities to spend time with the nearest tribal people, the Choctaws. She learned basket weaving and beading from the grandmas at the Choctaw Nation Capitol Museum in Tuskahoma. Additionally, her adoptive father, who operated a little country store, often donated materials to the women at the museum so they could make ribbon shirts, Native dresses, and dance outfits.

Kimberly remembers that from an early age she felt a sense of purpose for her life as a bridge builder between Anglo and Native communities. That idea stayed with her as she grew and begin to get an education.

By second grade, she was already interested in performing in school plays, realizing that she was quite the "ham." Around that time, she saw a college football game on TV between two California teams, UCLA (University of California, Los Angeles) and USC (University of Southern California). When the screen showed the cheerleaders on the sideline with their gold-and-blue pom-poms, Kimberly announced to her family, "That's what I'm doing when I get older—I'm going to UCLA."

Brimming with ideas about performing, she was drawn to the idea of being on television. A quick review of a *Rand McNally Road Atlas* revealed to her that UCLA was right next door to the famous Beverly Hills and not far from the entertainment capital of the world, Hollywood. That confirmed it. She knew that was where she needed to be.

However, her parents had different ideas about her higher education, wanting her to begin her college career a little closer to home. This obstacle failed to deter the determined girl, and she began earnestly investigating other ways to achieve her goal.

That's when she discovered beauty pageants. A few national pageants offer a full college scholarship and a new car to the winner. Kimberly thought this would be the perfect way for her to get where she wanted to go. The only catch was that she had to win the contest to get the prize. Slim chance, right?

Her first step would be to enter the Miss Oklahoma Teen pageant in 1984.

"I had won a little pageant at my high school, so I knew how to act like the pageant girls on stage," she says. "Walk with grace, talk with grace, you know. That wasn't really me, but I could fake it."

Out of one hundred entries, Kimberly won that local pageant. Then it was on to the Miss National Teenager pageant, which would be televised and hosted by *Happy Days* television actor Anson Williams. Miracle of miracles, she won that one, too, complete with the full scholarship and a new small car!

It was Kimberly's brother who had convinced their parents to allow her to attend UCLA. "If she wins the scholarship and gets accepted to UCLA, you've got to let her go," he told them. "You've just got to trust her."

And so they did.

A series of decisions and guidance from a UCLA graduate led Kimberly to commit to acting as her chosen path into the entertainment industry. For the time being, while she was in college, she did actually become a "pom-pom girl" as a freshman, just as she had declared all those years before in Oklahoma.

As if Kimberly's story didn't already sound like an unlikely fairy tale, a casting director saw her at one of the UCLA basketball games and invited her to audition for an AT&T commercial to be broadcast on national television. Kimberly admits that she didn't know how to audition or know much of anything about the process.

However, once again she was selected and appeared in the commercial. After that TV spot began to air across the country, the aspiring actress discovered residuals, which are payments made to actors each time a national commercial is shown. She received a total of ten or eleven thousand dollars in residuals over the next couple of years.

Kimberly was immediately faced with another decision: Should she focus on acting or finish her college degree? After carefully weighing her options, she committed to finishing her degree. That's when she decided to major in history and create her own subcategory in Native American history.

After four years at UCLA, Kimberly got her bachelor's degree in history in 1989, clearly thinking of a fallback career in case acting didn't pan out for her. However, she actually put some of her historical research skills to work during her early acting jobs.

Kimberly portraying Cherokee Chief Wilma Mankiller in the feature film *The Cherokee Word for Water*.

In 1990, a groundbreaking major motion picture called *Dances with Wolves* hit movie screens worldwide. No other film since 1970's *Little Big Man* had really portrayed Native Americans as human beings. Kimberly wasn't in that movie but says that *Dances with Wolves* made Indians cool in the early 1990s, so many guest-starring roles began opening up on television.

One of the agencies in Los Angeles that was helping more Native actors find work at that time was a nonprofit organization called the American Indian Registry for the Performing Arts. The group, established in 1983 by Native actor Will Sampson and others, published a directory of Native actors, producers, directors, and technicians. Kimberly was included in that directory, which helped her get noticed by casting directors.

The first opportunity to come along after Kimberly's graduation was a two-part historical television miniseries called *Son of the Morning Star*. The project tells the story of George Armstrong Custer, leading up to the famous historical Battle of the Little Bighorn. Two points of view are presented, one by the wife of Custer and the other by a Cheyenne woman named Kate Bighead.

Kimberly researched the Cheyenne culture, history, and language quite extensively as part of her preparation for auditioning for the role of Kate Bighead. This included learning a few lines in the Cheyenne language that she got from a friend who is a member of that tribe.

Kimberly remembers the story of her audition for that role, which took place in a room filled with the film's producers as well as the director.

"They said, 'The cavalry is coming to attack your village and your family, so show us how you'd react,'" she recounts. "I just buried myself in that character and in that setting and went for it. I began yelling the Cheyenne phrases my friend taught me, expressing total fear and horror. By the time my performance was over, I was hiding underneath the director's desk."

She recalls thinking that she had either freaked out every-one in that room or she had nailed the character. Turns out, she nailed it and got that part, which was her first television role. This was followed by a role as a guest star in an episode of *Northern Exposure* and a part in the TV movie *Geronimo.*

One of the key factors that Kimberly says helped her so much when she was just starting out in acting was the guid-ance and encouragement she received from a group of mentors, people who have had some experience in the industry. Her list of mentors includes UCLA graduate and entertainment execu-tive Danelle Black; Native musician, activist, and actor John Trudell; Native actor and artist Ray Tracey; and Cana-dian Indigenous actor Tantoo Cardinal. Each in their own way provided a crash course on the inner workings of the industry.

So it's not surprising that, in 1993, when Kimberly got the chance to audition for a part in the hit TV series *Seinfeld,* she felt ready. The episode, titled "The Cigar Store Indian," was part of the show's fifth season, and it purposefully played around with cringe-worthy Native American stereotypes.

A lot of familiar Native female actors, many with more act-ing experience, showed up for the first round of auditions, just as she had expected. And there was also the usual collection of young women who could "play Native" because of their brown eyes, dark hair, and brownish skin. Several of these came in their buckskin outfits and even feathered headdresses because that's what they thought Native women still looked like!

After the first round of auditions, Kimberly and three oth-ers got callbacks, meaning they were the only ones still being considered for the part. She decided to do this audition as an "in-your-face" modern Native American New Yorker, the kind of woman that Jerry Seinfeld's TV character might go for. After doing the reading in front of the show's creator, Larry David, along with Jerry Seinfeld and a dozen other executives, she got the part.

Shortly after doing the *Seinfeld* show, Kimberly landed an ongoing part as a Native character in the popular daytime

Kimberly takes a break during filming.

soap opera *As the World Turns*. Unbeknownst to her, this show was also popular with some Native grandmas out on the reservations. On the Lower Brule reservation in South Dakota, these grandmas were particularly excited about a Native character appearing on their favorite show.

Consequently, the tribe invited Kimberly to come to the rez to speak to the youth. And they asked her to come back and speak several times about issues the youth were facing. Being a motivational speaker for Native youth became an important part of Kimberly's work, which she continued between acting gigs.

With the help of other collaborators, that activity grew into the Akatubi Film and Music Academy for Native youth. That group included Indigenous American director Randy Redroad and Sicangu Lakota producer Yvonne Russo, along with Kimberly's musician husband, Johnny Guerrero, whom she married in 1996. Together, they taught acting classes on different reservations, along with video production and music recording, for several years.

Moving beyond the realm of entertainment and production, Akatubi Film and Music Academy also worked with Native youth to improve their employability and social skills. After being coached through videotaped interviews, the young people's self-confidence increased along with their ability to talk effectively with authority figures and potential employers.

In 2007, Kimberly was called to audition in Chicago for a role in *August: Osage County*, a new play about the toxic and tumultuous life of a non-Indian family in Pawhuska, Oklahoma. The young actor initially turned down the offer to audition for the part of Johnna due to recent losses in her own family. A persistent casting director convinced her to make the trip and conduct the audition as best she could. In spite of her emotional state, Kimberly aced the audition and got the part. After the play's successful run with the Steppenwolf Theater group in Chicago, the production moved to New York City, where it played on Broadway. The following year, the play won a Tony Award and the Pulitzer Prize for Drama.

The original cast, including Kimberly, traveled to England to present the play at the National Theatre in London and then went to Australia to perform it at the Sydney Theatre Company.

As the years passed, Kimberly continued her acting career in television and movies but still felt the strong pull to visit rural reservation communities to positively impact the lives of Native youth.

In 2013, Kimberly had a chance to combine both of those worlds, in a way, when she was picked to play the role of Wilma Mankiller in the feature film *The Cherokee Word for Water.* Set in the 1980s, the movie tells the true story of a small community coming together to improve their living conditions, including the installation of a twenty-mile waterline. The effort was led and organized by Mankiller, who later went on to become the first woman chief of the Cherokee Nation.

"It was a true honor to play such a powerful Native woman who did so much for her people," Kimberly says. "Wilma Mankiller's impact was felt throughout Indian Country, and she was a role model for all young Native women."

Not long after that project, Kimberly joined Randy Redroad and her husband, Johnny Guerrero, on the Coeur d'Alene reservation in Idaho to shoot another powerful project. Their mission was to produce a music video about historical trauma in Native communities. The finished piece, titled *We Shall Remain,* was based on a song for which Kimberly and Randy wrote the lyrics and Johnny composed the music. After they posted the film on YouTube in August 2014, the response was incredible. The video attracted thousands of views, and the team decided they should formalize their working relationship by giving their group a name. That's when the StyleHorse Collective was born. Simply put, the creative group's purpose is to tell stories (through digital media and music) about tribes, for tribes.

Seeing the impact StyleHorse Collective was having among Native people, Kimberly realized it was time to begin the next chapter of her life and career. She returned to college to study screenwriting and earned her master's degree in that field in 2017.

Getting that degree did two things for her: it gave her experience in writing for television and film and also provided the credentials she needed to begin teaching at the university level. Now, Professor Kimberly Guerrero is teaching at the University of California, Riverside in the Department of Theater, Film, and Digital Production.

Kimberly's life has become a whirlwind of activity: writing and pitching television pilots and movies, producing positive programs for and about tribes, teaching acting at the university, and, of course, acting.

When someone tells her, "My, but you're busy," she answers, "Yeah, but I'm not complaining."

SELECT FILMOGRAPHY

2020: *The Glorias* (feature film); Wilma Mankiller

2019: *Shadow Wolves* (feature film); Naomi

2014: *We Shall Remain* (music video); writer, producer (StyleHorse Collective)

2013: *The Cherokee Word for Water* (feature film); Wilma Mankiller

2012–2014: *Longmire* (TV series); Neena Wapasha/Joanna

2004: *Hidalgo* (feature film); Frank's mother

2003: *Dreamkeeper* (TV movies); Pretty woman

1998: *Naturally Native* (feature film); Karen Lewis

1996: *Raven Hawk* (TV movie); Rhyia's mother

1993: *Seinfeld* episode #74 (NBC comedy series); Winona

1992–1993: *As the World Turns* (TV series); Simone Bordeau

1991: *Son of the Morning Star* (TV miniseries); Kate Bighead

Michael Horse

YAQUI ACTOR

Michael Horse is one of the best-known and busiest Native American actors in the entertainment industry. Many people recognize him from one or more of his ninety-plus television and movie roles.

Born in Los Angeles of Yaqui, Hispanic, and Swedish descent, Michael didn't grow up wanting to be an actor. Music and art were more his style. As a kid, he took frequent trips with his family to Arizona and Sonora, Mexico, where he was exposed to those activities, along with his Yaqui roots. In addition, Michael learned how to ride and take care of horses.

Consequently, as a young man living in Los Angeles, he was able to get work wrangling horses for movies. One day at work, he was asked if he could ride a horse across the desert, shoot a gun, and fall off like he'd been shot. Michael's immediate response was, "I fall off *and* I get paid? I've been in the wrong end of this deal. I've been trying to stay on!" He then began working as a stunt performer, doing bit parts in films part-time.

While he was working with horses and doing stunts, Michael was also pursuing a career as an artist. He ended up renting an art studio from a woman who happened to be a talent agent. In 1980, the agent asked Michael if he wanted to play the character Tonto in a new movie called *The Legend of*

47

Michael Horse.

the Lone Ranger. The Tonto role had been played and made famous by Mohawk actor Jay Silverheels, who had starred in the popular television series *The Lone Ranger* from 1949 to 1957.

Michael wasn't really interested in full-scale acting and initially declined the agent's offer. Historically, Native Americans had not been portrayed accurately or favorably in movies, so this was a very real concern for him and other Native people at the time. He decided he didn't want to be a part of that. However, once the agent told the reluctant actor how much the job paid, Michael, the starving artist, decided that he should at least meet the movie's director before turning down the offer completely.

William A. Fraker, who would be directing the movie, had coincidentally served as a camera operator on *The Lone Ranger*

TV series and had already directed one other western. In that meeting, the director assured Michael that Tonto would be portrayed honorably and with dignity. And so his unexpected acting career began.

"I never meant to be in the acting business as long as I have," he says. "I'm a jeweler and a painter. That was my passion, and that was going to be my profession. The whole acting thing happened by accident."

In the 1980s, after the Tonto role, Michael got several small television roles and movie parts with a few performances that make him cringe when he looks back and sees them now.

"I wasn't really very good as an actor then, and the parts I played weren't that good either," Michael says.

But then, in 1989, an opportunity to work on an innovative and quirky TV series called *Twin Peaks* came to him out of the blue. Director David Lynch gave Michael the part of Deputy Chief Tommy "Hawk" Hill in the show, which was about the murder of a teenager in a small town.

"That was a big break for me," Michael says, "because it was a really interesting role. That character did away with some of the Indian stereotypes in those days. Also, that series became known for its impact on all of television programming. So many TV and movie creators pointed to the influence that series had on them."

Because that series became so well respected within the film and television production community, Michael's status as an actor improved. He started to receive offers for more desirable parts in TV and movie projects with bigger budgets, higher ratings, and better reviews. But Michael says that no matter how good the ratings are or how popular a show is, being an Indigenous actor can be challenging. So much of what non-Native directors, writers, and producers have created about Native Americans in the past was stereotypical, inaccurate, and just plain wrong.

"You'd like to be able to pick and choose the parts you play and the roles you take," Michael says. "But if you wait for the perfect part in a movie that portrays Indians properly, you may only get hired to act once every ten years."

That's the advice the Muscogee-Creek Indian actor Will Sampson gave Michael back then. The two had become friends, and Will had been nominated for an Academy Award for Best Supporting Actor for his role as Chief Bromden in the 1975 feature film *One Flew Over the Cuckoo's Nest*. That movie won five Academy Awards, including Best Picture, Best Director, and Best Screenplay.

In addition to *Twin Peaks*, *North of 60* was another of Michael's favorite television series. The title refers to the geographic location where the series took place: north of 60 degrees latitude in Canada. Unfortunately, viewers in the United States never got to see that groundbreaking show, which ran six years on Canadian TV.

"It was a wonderful prime-time Native TV show," Michael says. "It was about Indigenous people trying to hold on to their culture and their children—a real joy to be a part of."

One thing that made it so great and so real, Michael added, were the Indigenous writers, directors, and actors who worked on the show. "They seemed to make all the difference in the quality and accuracy of the stories being told in the series."

Voice-over work for animation is another genre that Michael has had an opportunity to participate in. And he loves it! He says Native actors excel in doing voice-overs because "we come from storytelling peoples."

"Before movies or TV or even radio, we were storytellers," he says.

What animation projects has he worked on? He rattles them off: *Rugrats, Captain Planet, Superman, Batman,* and *The Real Adventures of Johnny Quest*—just to name a few!

His favorite, though, is *Spirit: Stallion of the Cimarron,* an animated movie produced in 2002. It's the story of a wild stallion that is captured by humans but never gives up the hope of one day returning to his herd. The lead voice actor was Matt Damon, and other Native actors on the project included Zahn McClarnon and Daniel Studi.

Michael thinks Native actors have a duty to speak up about stereotypical roles they are asked to play or suggest changes to dialogue that more accurately reflect who American Indians are as people.

"Sometimes they [directors/producers] listen, sometimes they don't," Michael says. "Many non-Native filmmakers and even viewers don't necessarily want to know the truth about us. They often have their own romanticized, fantasy version of Indians in their minds, and they don't want that image ruined by reality. As a Native actor, you have to make a hard choice. Do you take a job because you need the cash and the screen credit, or do you turn down a job that you know doesn't reflect the truth about our community?"

Nevertheless, thinking back on his forty-five-year acting career, Michael has seen some positive changes. He says that back in the 1950s and 1960s, the way Native people were characterized was outrageously bad. But mainstream society has become more conscious of how minority communities and individuals are portrayed. That goes not just for Native Americans but also Asian Americans, Latinos, and other groups.

Another positive change he's seen is an increase in the number of Native writers, directors, and producers breaking into the business and getting hired.

"It's not like a non-Native person isn't a great filmmaker or storyteller, but if you're doing a story about a culture that's different from your own, then you need to bring in someone from that culture to guide you," he says. "Otherwise, you're going to skew that story in the wrong direction because you just don't know any better."

Michael points to one example of an incredible feature film written, produced, directed, and acted by predominantly

Indigenous people: the 2002 production of *The Fast Runner*. It was based on a thousand-year-old story told and retold among the Inuit people for generations. The film was shot in the Inuit language in the frozen landscape of the Arctic Circle, reviewed and approved by tribal elders, and ultimately applauded by audiences worldwide.

"I have friends who are non-Native filmmakers, and they think it's the most amazing film they've ever seen," Michael says. "It's a great film for young filmmakers to study and learn from."

Michael believes there are many ways in which the work of an actor is very different from a full-time, nine-to-five job, and there are some ways that it's the same.

"It's a job," he explained. "It's a hard job, and it can be a long, tedious job, but it's a job nonetheless. So you have to learn the craft and how to be a complete professional about it."

Many young people see movies and TV shows and think about how glamorous it all seems, but when you begin working in the industry, you realize how much effort is involved and how hard everybody works. "You must have a good work ethic to make it," Michael says.

Michael goes on to point out that, in addition to the actors you see on the screen, there are so many people working behind the scenes that the audience never sees: the people who drive the trucks, do the makeup and wardrobe, build sets, and the list goes on and on. It takes an incredible number of people all working together to make a large-scale movie.

"And they all deserve respect for what they do because without them you wouldn't be able to do your job as an actor," he says.

Michael's wife, who recently joined him on a film set to watch him work, was impressed with how hard acting can be. Michael had to do about twenty takes for one small scene before the director was happy with it.

Michael (right) on the set of an action film.

"I don't know how you do that over and over again and make it look like the first time, every time," she commented afterward. Michael replied, "That's the job. That's what you've got to do."

One of Michael's recent acting jobs was for a remake of *The Call of the Wild*, based on a famous book written by Jack London. The story is set in the 1890s during the Klondike Gold Rush. The first movie version was produced in 1935. Since then, other filmmakers have produced other versions. The most recent remake (2020) stars Harrison Ford. Michael Horse plays an Indigenous Canadian character named Edenshaw.

"I think this is some of the best work I've ever done," Michael says. "I'm a big fan of writing, and a big fan of Jack London's work, and this project was very well written. It's most faithful to the original book."

One thing that sets acting apart from a regular full-time job that requires you to work forty hours a week, every week, is the pay. Actors must go to auditions, which are called "readings," and compete with other actors to get a part. Then, if they're lucky enough to land a role, they must work whatever days and hours are required. When they finish one acting gig, they have to wait for another opportunity to come along, and then audition for that part.

Actors only get paid when they are working, so they have to have a backup plan, a job to fall back on between acting jobs. Many actors are also waiters, bartenders, or Uber or Lyft drivers.

"I've been very lucky because of my well-established art career," Michael says. "My work shows in galleries in Santa Fe and Los Angeles and other areas where Native American art is popular."

When young people ask Michael how to get into acting, he tells them to start with theater. "Theater is the best way to do it," he advises. "Do high school theater, college theater, or community theater. This is a very good way to practice the techniques of memorizing lines and performing on cue. It's also a good way of being seen by talent agents and casting directors."

The hardest parts of this business are getting an agent and getting into the union, the Screen Actors Guild (SAG). Both are necessary, but it's difficult to get into the union without experience, and it's difficult to get experience without belonging to the union. That's just the reality of the entertainment business.

But there are agents who will go to see plays if they're looking for new talent. If you're in the right place at the right time, an agent might spot you and offer to represent you for an upcoming film or TV project.

Because being an actor is the most visible aspect of the entertainment business, many young people target that job. But, according to Michael, not everyone is cut out for acting. If you want to be involved in the process, there are plenty of other jobs that need talented people, such as set directors and designers, set builders, stunt people, special-effects artists, and technicians, sound engineers, and camera assistants. Watch the end credits of any movie to see a comprehensive list.

Michael says that when you watch a movie or TV show, don't just pay attention to the actors. Look at everything in each scene. Somebody had to find the location, design the costumes, create the sound effects, or wrangle the horses.

And if you're very, very lucky, maybe one day someone will ask you to ride a horse across the desert, shoot a gun, fall off the horse, *and get paid!*

SELECTED FILMOGRAPHY

2020: *The Call of the Wild* (movie); Edenshaw

2019: *Claws* (TV series, 8 episodes); Mac Lovestone/Mac Locklear

2017: *Twin Peaks* (TV series, 14 episodes); Deputy Chief Tommy "Hawk" Hill

2002: *Spirit: Stallion of the Cimarron* (animated movie); Little Creek's friend (voice)

1995–1997: *North of 60* (Canadian TV series, 19 episodes); Andrew One Sky

1994: *Lakota Woman: Siege at Wounded Knee* (TV movie); Dennis Banks

1993: *The Untouchables* (TV series, 19 episodes); Agent George Steelman

1989: *Legend of 'Seeks-To-Hunt-Great'* (short film)

1989–1991: *Twin Peaks* (TV series, 28 episodes); Deputy Chief Tommy "Hawk" Hill

1985: *Knight Rider* (TV series); Jonathan Eagle

1981: *The Legend of the Lone Ranger* (movie); Tonto

Jack Kohler

HUPA ACTOR, PRODUCER, DIRECTOR, EDUCATOR

Jack Kohler, a member of the Hupa tribe with Yurok and Karuk blood, is among a small group of Native Americans who have excelled at being actors and filmmakers, but Jack is also an educator who is teaching those skills to younger Native people.

Born in San Francisco in 1961, Jack credits his grandmother with teaching him about his tribal roots. She was a great storyteller with a knack for humor, as was Jack's father, who worked for a large engineering and construction firm in San Francisco building skyscrapers. Both contributed to the boy's early exposure to storytelling.

However, Jack's parents had what he calls a "tumultuous marriage," so from ages one to

Jack Kohler.

seven, the boy lived with his grandparents. When Jack was around five years old, his grandfather had a stroke that affected the elderly man's ability to function or speak for the rest of his life.

One day, when Jack was about seven years old, his grandfather was sitting as usual in his La-Z-Boy chair, quietly watching television as Jack played with his toy cars on the living room floor. Suddenly, the elder stood up and declared, "Jackie, one day you're going to Stanford University," and then he sat back down.

"That's the only thing he ever said to me," Jack recalls. (Stanford University is a highly respected California college known for science and engineering excellence.)

As one of only two Native American students in his high school, Jack experienced quite a bit of prejudice. White students made fun of him, calling him "Tonto" or "Geronimo," terms that were meant to humiliate him.

As a senior in high school, Jack remembers a counselor giving him an application to attend a local state college, saying, "I think you'll do well at this school." Jack suddenly remembered what his grandfather had said all those years ago and told the counselor he wanted to go to Stanford instead. The counselor told him that he "wasn't Stanford material," meaning that he wasn't smart enough to go to a school like that.

Jack took the initiative to contact Stanford on his own and request the necessary application forms. He was accepted to this prestigious university and ended up being the *only* student from his high school chosen to go there.

While attending Stanford, Jack met other Native American students and started taking part in Native activities. That's when he began to feel the pride of being a Native American. During school breaks, he visited his grandmother and asked questions about his Native heritage. He also began attending events on his reservation at least once a year.

Jack Kohler as Tecumseh in 1996.

It was during his years at Stanford that Jack became interested in theater, after meeting Megan Chesnut, who was in the theater department.

"She really taught me about acting," Jack said. "How to present myself, how to project, how to be on stage. She cast me in a show during my senior year. That's when I got the theater bug."

Jack and Megan later married.

After graduation, Jack found a job using his engineering degree. But that job kept him cooped up in an office all day looking at blueprints and calculating the stress loads of buildings. He knew he couldn't do that for the rest of his life, so he quit and got a contractor's license to start his own business.

For the next eighteen years, he built high-rise apartment buildings in the San Francisco area, similar to what his father had been doing. That ended in bankruptcy when the owner of a large home Jack was building stopped paying for the construction. It turned out that the man, who was conducting illegal business operations, owed millions of dollars to banks. Consequently, his unfinished home, his funds, and all his belongings were confiscated by law-enforcement agencies.

Those events forced Jack to shut down his business, and it was at that point he realized he really didn't want to keep doing construction for the rest of his life anyway. That's when he finally began exploring music, film, and theater. He spent more time with his Native relatives, who encouraged him to work in these fields. Around 1994, Jack landed a part in a Native American play in the San Francis-

Jack Kohler in the production of *P.T. Survival D* in 2013.

co area about his own tribe. The play was called *Watershed* and was written by Stephen Most, an area screenwriter and playwright.

Participating in that stage production made Jack even more interested in the history and culture of his own people. He got more roles in other plays in the Bay Area and continued to improve as an actor as well.

In 1999, Stephen asked Jack to begin working on a documentary film about the Klamath River and the importance of the salmon to the Native peoples of that region, which are Jack's own people. That project, *River of Renewal*, took ten years to produce and chronicled the conflict between farmers, commercial fishers, and the tribes that had sustained themselves from the river for thousands of years.

This was the beginning of Jack's filmmaking career. But, like so many other actors and filmmakers, he continued to work a day job to pay bills. In Jack's case, that job was construction, working for other contractors.

In 2003, Mike Smith, of the American Indian Film Institute in San Francisco, hired Jack to teach ten-day video-production workshops for tribal youth. For three summers, Jack traveled to Indian reservations and taught screenwriting, videography, and editing—and he loved doing it. This process helped young Native people tell their own stories using the latest technology.

He also took on other short-term production projects, including *California's Lost Tribes*, a documentary piece that goes behind the scenes of the American Indian tribal gaming business. Jack, who was the project's coproducer, set up all the interviews with tribes and learned a lot about both gaming and filmmaking during that time. This film was shown on PBS stations in 2006.

"The *River of Renewal* film was finally completed and aired on PBS in 2009," Jack says. "For a long time it was the most watched Native American documentary to appear on PBS, having been shown two thousand times over the years."

Jack says that a film project like *River of Renewal* goes beyond simple entertainment. Sometimes a film can become an important communication tool that clearly explains how a public issue is affecting tribal people.

"That was one of the major reasons for getting this documentary completed," Jack says. "People needed to understand all the issues and how dams on the river were affecting water quality for all the tribes along the river. So I was strongly motivated to get it done because it would benefit a lot of Native people."

Another motivating factor for Jack to be involved with these particular film projects was the chance to work with experienced filmmakers who could teach him more about the craft of filmmaking.

"Collaboration, I found, is a great way to learn and also to get a film done," he says. "You can get a project finished a lot faster if you collaborate with somebody who has more resources and more advanced skills."

While he was still working on *River of Renewal*, Jack had the idea of creating a nonprofit educational media organization that could teach young Native people about production and give them some on-the-job training. He called the organization On Native Ground. Jack explains that the process of creating a nonprofit organization requires following certain federal guidelines, and these guidelines allow a self-governing tribe to issue a license to operate a nonprofit.

"It wasn't until 2011 that we officially got the tribal license to form On Native Ground," Jack says. "That allowed us time to seek grants to fund the organization's activities."

One of their first activities was to shoot the Sundance Film Festival's red-carpet events. Several students learned how to conduct on-camera interviews with actors and filmmakers and received firsthand experience in Park City, Utah, the location of the annual festival.

One of the organization's goals is to give Native peoples the skills needed to produce documentary and news footage about tribes, because so much of that has been done by non-Natives who don't have any understanding of Native cultures or tribal government operations.

Among the organization's ongoing series is *On Native Ground Youth Reports*, which has won four Native American Journalists Association National Native Media Awards for television excellence. The programs highlight tribal and entertainment news and feature interviews with positive Native role models. All the on-camera reporting and interviews are conducted by Native youth who are learning the various skills needed to produce TV programs.

"We've had several students who have gone on to attend colleges and film schools," Jack says. "Their experience with On Native Ground gives them a much-needed edge that will help them excel in their careers, whatever they choose to pursue."

In addition to the television news series, the organization has produced several short narrative films featuring both Native and non-Native actors. These projects provide students with real hands-on experience behind the scenes on location, in studios, and in the editing room.

On Native Ground also created opportunities for Native actors to launch acting careers through their projects. One such example is actor Martin Sensmeier.

"I recruited this young man from Washington State to play a major role in a film we did called *K'ina Kil: The Slaver's Son*," Jack explains. "Set during California's gold rush, the film is about how miners would kidnap young Native women. It's basically a true story about human trafficking. Martin used his scenes in the film to help him get cast in the movies *The Magnificent Seven* and then *Wind River*."

Another major accomplishment of On Native Ground was the production of the feature film *Behind the Door of a Secret Girl* in 2014. The project began as a three-page idea written by Janessa Starkey, a ninth-grade tribal schoolgirl. Through Jack's mentorship and guidance, she learned about screen-

Jack Kohler at the Native American Music Awards in 2018.

writing by turning her three-page idea into a ninety-eight-page movie script.

The story is about a Native high school girl who is secretly cutting herself as a way of coping with her dysfunctional home life. That includes a meth-addicted mother and the mother's drug-dealing boyfriend. It's a very sophisticated story based on an all-too-common reality.

"We shot the film during the summer between Janessa's junior and senior years in high school," Jack says. "We hired a few professional actors and a couple of professional crew people, but the rest of the crew members were all high school kids."

The movie won fifteen film festival awards around the United States.

The most ambitious project of On Native Ground was undoubtedly the 2016 musical stage production *Something Inside Is Broken*, the true story of the pre–gold rush destruction and enslavement of the Nisenan Indian people by John Sutter in the 1840s. Written, composed, and directed by Jack Kohler, this Native American rock opera was performed in several California cities and nearby states.

Although the main storyline of the play has a melancholy tone, there are some uplifting elements that include a celebration of the Indigenous Nisenan language, in which half of the show's sixteen original songs are performed.

The play received financial support from an online campaign through GoFundMe, as well as several tribal sponsors, including the Rincon Band of Luiseño Indians and the Tuolumne Band of Me-Wuk Indians.

In 2018, a feature-length movie version of the production was created, along with an audio recording of the original cast performing all of the show's songs.

Ever the mentor and educator, Jack offers one piece of advice to young people considering a career in acting or filmmaking: "You can do anything you want in life as long as you stick with it until the end and finish it. Giving up is not an option."

SELECTED FILMOGRAPHY

2018: *Something Inside Is Broken* (stage production/video); writer, producer, director, actor

2017: *The Land of Little Big* (TV movie); writer, producer, director, actor

2016: *Standing Rock on Native Ground* (documentary); producer, editor

2014: *Behind the Door of a Secret Girl* (feature film); writer, producer, director, editor

2012–2013: *On Native Ground* (TV series); writer, producer, director, editor

2012: *Joseph's War Pony* (short film); actor

2009: *River of Renewal* (documentary); producer

2005: *California's Lost Tribes* (documentary); producer

1996: *Grand Avenue* (HBO movie); actor

1994: *Watershed* (play); actor

Doreen Manuel

SECWEPEMC/KTUNAXA PRODUCER, DIRECTOR, EDUCATOR

Born into a family destined to change the course of Canadian Indigenous history, Doreen lived first on the Neskonlith Indian Band reserve in the interior of British Columbia. Her grandparents were traditional healers and storytellers who influenced her early years and introduced her to the concept of communicating with spirits to get guidance in her life.

Her mother, Marceline Paul, and her grandmother, Mary Paul, got the young girl started on traditional beading, a Native artistic expression Doreen has continued into her adult life. By age twelve, she was sewing to transform clothing bought at secondhand stores into something more fashionable.

Her father, Grand Chief Dr. George Manuel, was a major figure in the political fight for Canadian and worldwide Indigenous peoples' rights. Doreen's mother, Marceline, was an influential cultural and spiritual leader among Canadian First Nations people who also participated in that struggle from a different angle.

During the late 1960s and early 1970s, Doreen's mother and siblings got actively involved in what many people called the Red Power Movement, which sought to improve laws, policies, and living conditions for Indigenous people in the

Doreen Manuel.

United States and Canada. Doreen saw firsthand groups such as the American Indian Movement (AIM) and the Aboriginal women's movement address these issues directly with mass protests, caravans across the country, and takeovers of government buildings.

She considers all these strands of cultural, spiritual, and political life experiences to be important parts of her total personal education. In the academic realm, because of changing interests and changing majors, it took her almost twenty years to earn a college bachelor's degree. That included courses in all the major forms of art as well as some business management, psychology, and public administration courses.

But her introduction to the world of film and video production didn't occur until the late 1990s, when she was asked to establish a Native school for a tribe in Idaho. Many of the students there expressed an interest in learning how to make movies.

Doreen contacted a Kootenay cousin who had been using video equipment to interview tribal elders in order to preserve oral histories and cultures. He brought his equipment to the school and spent one day showing the students how the process worked. The second day, they shot a short video about a family who raised a wolf pup.

That experience so impressed Doreen that, after she finished her work at that school and returned to Canada, she felt that studying film production might be a path for her. After much thought and prayer about what she would do next with her life, she was miraculously offered free tuition to go to film school at Capilano University in North Vancouver, British Columbia.

At this university, she took classes through the Aboriginal Film and Television Program (now named the Indigenous Independent Digital Filmmaking Program), which was run by a non-Native director. Although Doreen graduated from the program, during her studies there, she had observed several problems in the whole way the program was conducted. After Doreen's graduation, the director told her the program had a high dropout rate, and he asked for her input on what he could do to fix that.

"You don't have any Native culture in the program," she told him. "You've set it up to be very competitive, very cutthroat. It should include Native cultural values, which would take a more cooperative approach."

He asked her to develop a course outline based on her suggestions, and then he got the outline approved by the university administration. Doreen was asked to teach the course the following fall, and she continued to teach it for two years.

In order to pay her bills, she also held other positions, including working as the director for Aboriginal Peoples Television Network and as an assistant director for a small studio.

Then Doreen returned full-time to Capilano University, fondly known as CapU to students and faculty, to become the coordinator of the program she had graduated from two years earlier. At that point, she mainly focused on helping students produce their school film projects, which left her with little time or energy to write, produce, and direct her own films.

In 2012, Doreen was invited to enter a local eight-day film competition in Vancouver known as Crazy8s (Crazy Eights). Begun in 1999, the annual event provides emerging film-makers an opportunity to create a fully funded short film that will be presented to film professionals in the area. The competition had never previously involved any Indigenous filmmakers. Doreen won that year's competition with her original piece *These Walls*, about the babies that were buried within the walls of one of Canada's residential schools for First Nations students.

Shortly after that experience, she entered the master's degree program at the University of British Columbia and, in 2014, created a documentary called *Freedom Babies* as a student project. The film follows Doreen's niece Kanahus over the course of a year as she raises her children free of the effects of colonization and the restrictions of the Canadian government in an effort to preserve their culture and protect Native lands.

It was during these times that Doreen began to experiment with what she calls "spirit communication" in song and prayer before starting to write or direct a film. One particular experience stands out in her mind that demonstrated spiritual support was present.

Doreen takes a break between setups.

On the last day of location production, before shooting the final scene, she described to her actress what action was needed. Doreen told the woman to look up, as if she'd just heard a sound, and stare into the sky with an expression of hope on her face. The experienced actress had exhibited a dismissive attitude toward Doreen during the shoot because the woman considered the director to be green and inexperienced. She responded to Doreen's request with that same attitude, asking her what kind of sound she was supposed to be hearing.

Doreen answered, "It's a spirit sound," to which the actress asked, "So what does that sound like?" Doreen said, "It sounds like a cross between an eagle whistle blowing and a whoosh sound." The actress wasn't sure what that sound really was, but she agreed to try to appear to be listening to it.

While her camera operator was getting ready for the shot, Doreen returned to her seat at the production monitor and suddenly a new Native song came into her mind. She thought to herself, "Wow! I've never heard that song before. I think a song just came to me." So she sang the song quietly to herself and recorded it on her phone.

Then the camera operator signaled that she was ready to begin, and Doreen called, "Action!" She watched the shot unfold on the video monitor and saw the actress perform exactly as she had directed her. Doreen thought, "Oh my god, she got it on the first take!" So she called, "Cut!" and rushed over to the actress to say, "You got it perfect! I love that take."

The actress replied, "I heard that sound you described, and I was so shocked. I heard it and looked up." Doreen thought to herself, "The spirits are on this set!" A few moments later, as she and the actress continued talking, a pair of eagles burst from the branches of a nearby tree only about ten feet away from them. The two birds were playfully flying and circling each other, then they flew straight toward Doreen and zoomed passed her. Finally, the pair circled the whole set and flew away. This sight astounded everyone on the set.

After they wrapped, the crew enjoyed a dinner that Doreen provided as part of her thank-you to everyone who worked on the film. The actress, very humbly, apologized for her attitude and behavior and then hugged Doreen.

"The films I get most passionate about producing, and have actually been producing, are stories that come somehow from the spirits," Doreen says. "Or they come through some spirit connection."

Doreen spent thirteen years as the head of the CapU program, now known as the Indigenous Independent Digital Filmmaking Program, overseeing student productions and not really having the time or energy to write and direct her own pieces. But all that hard work paid off, because in November 2018, she became the director of CapU's Bosa Centre for Film and Animation, the home of the university's School of Motion Picture Arts.

In the summer of 2019, Doreen was named Woman of the Year by Women in Film and Television Vancouver. She was recognized as "an inspiring leader and artist who has affected many with her films and mentorship."

But film production and education aren't the only activities Doreen has excelled at. She has been practicing several traditional Native arts all her life, having learned hide tanning, leatherwork, and beadwork from her grandmother and mother. Lately she's been creating award-winning beaded Converse running shoes.

In 2019, Doreen's beadwork won her the BC Achievement Foundation Fulmer Award in First Nations Art. The organization honors excellence and inspires achievement throughout British Columbia.

Doreen advises young people who are interested in the film business to go to film school. She says, "It's important to learn the solid basics of camera composition, production techniques, and all that, but focus on learning how to tell stories on-screen."

She believes that when Indigenous filmmakers are spiritually connected, they will receive help and support for their work. They will be empowered to understand which stories to share and how to share them.

"There are stories all around us that need to be told," she explains. "Stories are embedded in the ground we walk on, the air we breathe. They come from the trees and from nature all around us. But you have to connect to all that *spiritually* in order to hear it, to feel it."

Regarding filmed stories, Doreen is a strong believer in something she calls "story sovereignty," the concept that Native stories should be told by Native people. She feels that these film projects should be written, produced, directed, and crewed by Indigenous people.

"Something that really troubles me is when I see non-Indigenous filmmakers getting awards for their filmed Native stories," she said. "Because of their expertise and experience, they often get funding for an Indigenous project, funding that should have gone to an Indigenous filmmaker who may be less experienced or less well known."

Doreen believes that Native filmmakers need to work together to create Indigenous cinema. But she says that a truly Indigenous form of cinema can happen only when there are more Native producers, writers, directors, editors, and cinematographers who can incorporate traditional forms of Native storytelling into their approach to production.

Native filmmakers may learn the crafts of television and film production from members of mainstream media, but then they have to break away from the mainstream storytelling style.

"We have to stop at some point and step back to ask how our grandparents told stories," Doreen advises. "How can I weave a story like my grandparents did and evolve that into uniquely Indigenous cinema?"

An additional element of Indigenous cinema involves the production process itself. Doreen says that people on typical non-Native sets are angry, often yelling orders at one another. And they have a strict hierarchy that allows you to speak only to your direct supervisor and not to someone in another department. On top of that, crews have to work sixteen to eighteen hours a day in these harsh work environments.

The goal for Indigenous projects would be to work more collaboratively, allowing for a sense of shared ownership in the outcome. Respect for the project and for one another comes from beginning a shoot with a smudge or a prayer. This puts everyone in a calm frame of mind, helps defuse conflicts, and keep egos from taking over.

Today Doreen wears many hats, you could say, in addition to her position at Capilano University. She's on three diversity work groups that strive to increase the number of people from

Doreen became the director of Capilano University's Bosa Centre for Film and Animation in 2018.

minority communities working in television and film. One is with the Diversity Committee of the Canadian Media Producers Association. Another is Telefilm Canada, one of that nation's largest funding sources for movies and TV production.

Finally, Doreen is on the Indigenous Advisory Council for Storyhive, a funding body in British Columbia that provides grants for short films and supports local filmmakers. Her involvement has increased the number of Indigenous projects that get funded.

From Doreen's point of view, the future of filmmaking for First Nations people is opening up. More training programs and funding opportunities are giving Indigenous filmmakers a better chance at having their stories produced, their projects funded, and their voices heard.

SELECTED FILMOGRAPHY

2018: *Fifty Shades of Red* (short film); producer

2017: *Standing Rock Stories* (short film); producer

2015: *The Fast* (short film); writer, director

2014: *Freedom Babies* (documentary short); writer, producer, director

2013: *Lucky Spirits* (short film); writer, producer, director

2012: *These Walls* (short film); writer, director

2010: *Reserved for Hollywood* (short film); producer

Alanis Obomsawin

ABENAKI PRODUCER, DIRECTOR

S ometimes called the Mother of Indigenous Cinema, Abenaki filmmaker Alanis Obomsawin is certainly known as one of the most important filmmakers in Canada. Born in 1932 in the US state of New Hampshire, she was primarily raised in the province of Quebec, Canada.

During her early years, her life was filled with the stories, songs, and history of the Abenaki people, thanks to elder

Alanis Obomsawin.

relatives in her family. This profoundly affected her view of and approach to life in general and her style of filmmaking specifically.

In 1960, Alanis made her professional debut as a singer-songwriter. As a performer, she traversed Canada, Europe, and the United States. Many of her performances were benefits for humanitarian causes at folk festivals, museums, universities, and art centers. She made other appearances at schools across Canada to share the stories and songs of her tribal people.

Canada's National Film Board (NFB), a media production and distribution agency of the Canadian government, first noticed Alanis as the result of a successful fundraising concert she held in the mid-1960s in the Quebec town of Odanak. The goal of the event was to raise funds to build a swimming pool for nonwhite children, because the only pool in the city was strictly for white residents.

Portions of her performance and an interview with her were nationally broadcast. Producers from the NFB saw the broadcast, liked what they saw, and contacted her. Soon afterward, they invited the singer/storyteller to be an advise on a film about Indigenous Canadian people. That introduction to the film-production process convinced Alanis she could produce and direct her own films. She wanted to make films about Indigenous peoples, issues, and histories in a style that was more reflective of Native points of view.

Alanis directed her first film for the NFB in 1971. Titled *Christmas at Moose Factory*, the short film's imagery consists entirely of crayon drawings made by young Cree children. The project was filmed at a residential school in northern Ontario, where the children told short stories of their own lives and described the pictures they'd drawn. Moose Factory is an old settlement, mostly made up of Indigenous families, located on an island in the Moose River in the Cochrane District of Ontario, Canada. *Christmas at Moose Factory* focuses on the lives of Indigenous children, a theme Alanis returned to several times in her career.

At an early stage in her filmmaking career, this Abenaki director discovered that her most important role in the process was to listen—listen to people who were most often unheard, most often ignored. Her technique for getting Indigenous people to open up and speak to her in front of a camera was to first show up without the camera. The next step was to begin a dialogue that demonstrated that she paid attention to what they had to say. Then, after a relationship of trust was established, she brought the camera in to begin filming.

In 1972, her second short documentary, *History of Manawan: Part One*, was released. The words of an elder in the community told the history of that reserve, which had been created by the government only seventy years earlier.

"It's not how it used to be," the Native man says of the changes his people were forced to make at Manawan. Where once they practiced their customs freely within a vast territory, they were now made to live on this small piece of land and live their lives more like the European immigrants who had settled around them. A longing for their old Indigenous ways was evident in his voice.

Mother of Many Children was Alanis's first feature-length documentary, a film longer than one hour. Produced in 1977, it honors the central position women and mothers have within Indigenous societies. The film depicts the pressures placed on these women to adapt to the standards and expectations of the dominant society, a society that expects women to follow the wishes of men. Following the cycle of several Native women's lives from birth to childhood, puberty, adulthood, and old age, this unique project revealed how these women had fought to regain a feeling of equality. In the end, they were able to instill cultural pride in their children so that traditional stories, songs, and language could be passed on to future generations.

Alanis often says that her career as a filmmaker was about giving a microphone to the people whose voices had been

Alanis Obomsawin on location during one of her early productions.

silenced. This was proven in film after film as her work shared one hidden Indigenous story after another, many of which revealed the crushing social injustices heaped upon Indigenous communities.

In 1984, Alanis created her most potent and passionate film up to that point. *Incident at Restigouche* covered a Mi'kmaq (Micmac) community's fight to maintain and exercise its fishing rights in the face of police raids ordered by Canadian government officials. The film captures a confrontation between the filmmaker, seen on camera, and the Quebec minister of fisheries, who had ordered the police action. This production marks the moment when Alanis's filmmaking became an act of social protest. Audience reactions to the film confirmed to her the power of film as a tool for social justice.

Through the 1980s, the director continued to create powerful, socially relevant work that, in some cases, even led to laws being changed in order to correct unfair social situations. Her *Poundmaker's Lodge: A Healing Place* (1987) examines ways that systemic racism could lead to addiction, and *No Address* (1988) presents portraits of homeless Indigenous people in Montreal.

Because of those projects, Alanis was prepared like no other media maker for what was to happen next in Indigenous peoples' struggles for human rights. In the summer of 1990, she documented the armed standoff between Mohawk demonstrators, the Quebec police, and the Canadian army. Often called the Oka Crisis, the incident began as a land dispute between a group of Mohawk traditionalists who had claimed the property and the nearby town of Oka, Quebec. Oka town leaders planned to build a golf course and condominiums on the site without consulting the tribe.

When the conflict escalated to tear gas, concussion grenades, and gunfire, news media from around the world showed up to cover the unfolding events. However, as the threat of violence increased during the seventy-eight days of the ordeal, most media outlets began pulling their reporters and camera operators from the scene, fearing for their safety. Although the National Film Board asked Alanis to also leave, she and her crew stayed.

"It was history that needed to be recorded," she says. "I was going to tell the story until the end."

At one point, Alanis had to smuggle her videotapes out of the area to prevent them from being confiscated by the authorities. She spent all seventy-eight days filming the incident, and in 1993, her groundbreaking documentary *Kanehsatake: 270 Years of Resistance* was completed.

The whole affair forced changes in Canada's national policies regarding Indigenous peoples. Furthermore, Alanis's film brought her international attention, inspired a whole new generation of Indigenous documentary filmmakers, and set her status as one of the world's most important activist filmmakers.

In addition to using the voices of the people she films, Alanis often narrates her own productions. Her melodic voice provides soft yet compelling background information and an explanation of what viewers are witnessing on the screen.

That was the case when she started the production of *Our Nationhood*, a documentary about the Mi'kmaq people's fight to regain their hunting, fishing, and logging rights on their traditional lands. The film, which was released in 2003, documents the tribe's capability to successfully manage their own natural resources and portrays their ultimate victorious outcome.

Alanis's next project was the 2006 feature-length production *Waban-aki: People from Where the Sun Rises*. Winning that year's Best Documentary Award at the imagineNATIVE Film + Media Arts Festival held annually in Toronto, the film profiles Alanis's return for the first time in her career to the village where she was raised. Demonstrations of traditional tribal crafts and discussions of historic struggles to remain on the land are included to tell the story of her own people.

The 2016 production *We Can't Make the Same Mistake Twice* chronicles the historic discrimination suit filed against the government of Canada in 2007 by the First Nations Child and Family Caring Society of Canada and the Assembly of First Nations regarding the government's inequitable treatment of Indigenous children. Frontline childcare workers and experts took part in a ten-year court battle to ensure that these children received the same level of care as other Canadian children. In the film, Alanis's camera exposes generations of injustices faced by children who are living on government-mandated reserves.

Her work on that film and others brought her two honors that same year. In June, she was named a Grand Officer of the

Alanis discusses a shot with her location sound operator.

National Order of Quebec, one of the province's highest tributes. Then, in November, she was given a prestigious award by the Toronto Film Critics Association, which called Alanis a "significant architect of Canadian cinema and culture."

In 2019, Alanis completed her fifty-second film, *Jordan River Anderson, the Messenger*, which was part of a series of documentaries that examine the rights of Indigenous children and youth. This production brought the filmmaker full circle, back to where she started in 1972 with *Christmas at Moose Factory*, focusing on the lives of Indigenous children. The film received the Best Canadian Documentary Award at that year's Vancouver International Film Festival.

The impact of Alanis's work is so widely recognized that two filmmaking awards have been named after her. Each year since 2001, a group known as Cinema Politica has given out the Alanis Obomsawin Award for Commitment to Community and Resistance to a filmmaker whose work best explores current social justice issues. The annual imagineNATIVE Film + Media Arts Festival presents The Alanis Obomsawin Best Documentary Award each year to a deserving Indigenous filmmaker.

Alanis's work has also rightfully earned her many other awards and honors over the years outside the film industry, including several honorary university doctoral degrees and humanitarian awards. She earned Canada's most respected national honor by being inducted into the Order of Canada in 2019 at the highest level. Companions of the Order of Canada, the top level of the Order, are people who have demonstrated the highest degree of merit to the nation of Canada and humanity.

Alanis's connection to that uniquely Canadian agency, the National Film Board of Canada, greatly benefited her filmmaking career as well as the careers of a few other Indigenous Canadian filmmakers. Created in 1939 as an agency of the government of Canada, the NFB's initial mandate was to "make and distribute films designed to help Canadians in all parts of Canada understand the ways of living and the problems of Canadians in other parts."

Over the years, the agency's mandate was revised and refined to broaden the diversity of the content it produced. For example, a 1950 revision of the National Film Act removed any direct government intervention into the operation and administration of the NFB. Then, in the early 1970s, the agency began a process of decentralization, opening production centers in cities across Canada. Those changes are part of what opened the NFB's doors to Indigenous filmmakers such as Alanis.

There is no agency similar to the NFB within the United States that could provide adequate funding and distribution for independent Indigenous media makers. America's Corporation for Public Broadcasting (CPB) and its sister organization, the Public Broadcasting Service (PBS), are partly funded by Congress and partly by private sources. The national "patchwork" approach to production funding and resource access has proven to be a hindrance to Native American filmmakers.

It has only been through the small, underfunded agency now known as Vision Maker Media (formerly the Native American Public Broadcasting Consortium) that Native media makers have had a chance to obtain at least partial funding and access to a segment of the national audience with whom they are able to share their visions and unique Native stories.

Whether they are in the United States, Canada, or other places in the world, Indigenous filmmakers owe much to Native trailblazer Alanis Obomsawin for opening the eyes of funders, broadcasters, distributors, and viewers to the struggles and successes of Native peoples.

SELECTED FILMOGRAPHY

2019: *Jordan River Anderson, the Messenger* (documentary)

2017: *Our People Will Be Healed* (documentary)

2016: *We Can't Make the Same Mistake Twice* (documentary)

2014: *Trick or Treaty?* (documentary)

2013: *Hi-Ho Mistahey!* (documentary)

2010: *When All the Leaves Are Gone* (documentary short)

2006: *Waban-aki: People from Where the Sun Rises* (documentary)

2005: *Sigwan* (short film)

2003: *Our Nationhood* (documentary)

1998: *Spudwrench: Kahnawake Man* (documentary)

1993: *Kanehsatake: 270 Years of Resistance* (documentary)

1992: *Walker* (short film)

1987: *Poundmaker's Lodge: A Healing Place* (short film)

1986: *Richard Cardinal: Cry from a Diary of a Metis Child* (short film)

1984: *Incident at Restigouche* (documentary)

1979: *Canada Vignettes: Wild Rice Harvest Kenora* (documentary short)

1977: *Mother of Many Children* (documentary)

1972: *History of Manawan: Part One* (documentary short)

1971: *Christmas at Moose Factory* (documentary short)

Note to readers: Many of Alanis Obomsawin's films can be seen online at the NFB website: nfb.ca/directors/alanis-obomsawin.

Randy Redroad

**INDIGENOUS AMERICAN WRITER,
DIRECTOR, EDITOR**

Born in the mid-1960s, Randy Redroad grew up on the vast plains of West Texas in the midst of widespread prejudice from his white neighbors and classmates. Being a dark-skinned Native child, he became very familiar with all the racial insults any Mexican, Asian, or Indian person might have experienced in those days, in that place. In spite of that aspect of his young existence, the experiences of life on that wide-open land, with its jackrabbits, tumbleweeds, and frequent tornado warnings, seem to be deeply rooted in his soul, almost a part of his DNA.

Randy's Cherokee mother had been separated as an infant from her own family and culture. Her lifelong investigation into her and Randy's cultural roots eventually led them back to Tahlequah, Oklahoma, capital of the Cherokee Nation, and ancient tribal ceremonies, such as the Stomp Dance.

From an early age, Randy loved movies and the escape from reality they offered. The whole moviegoing experience— sitting in a movie theater or a drive-in to take part in thrilling

Note to readers: Randy had identified as Cherokee most of his life, based on his mother's family history and research. However, having no documented proof, he recently decided to identify simply as Indigenous American because that's all his DNA test could report.

Randy Redroad.

adventures of sight and sound displayed in larger-than-life images on the big screen—totally captivated him.

"I didn't know what a bad movie was when I was growing up," Randy says. "I saw *Smokey and the Bandit* [1977] and *Smokey and the Bandit II* (1980), and to me they were both masterpieces." Both of these films starred Burt Reynolds as Bandit, a freewheeling, lawbreaking folk hero who was pursued across several states by a state trooper known as Smokey.

He also remembers marveling as a kid at the Indiana Jones movies, such as *Raiders of the Lost Ark*. At the time, it seemed like the coolest thing ever. Later in life, though, Randy realized that the Indiana Jones character was basically a glorified grave robber. But back then, it was an overwhelming work of art combined with its sibling form of artistic expression, music. He says cinema and music were the two most powerful influences on him as a young person.

Right after Randy graduated from Lubbock High School, his divorced mother decided to move to New York City. Randy packed his things and went with her. He was in what he calls his "angry, young Native phase" then and was ready to leave Texas behind. In his imagination, New York was a hundred miles of concrete, almost like an alien planet in a science-fiction movie.

He ended up falling in love with the place and stayed for seventeen years. His first job was as a bike messenger, delivering packages all over the city. That lasted four years. He tried college for a semester, dropped out, and then took a ten-month filmmaking workshop at a place called Third World Newsreel. The mission of that media-arts organization is to support people of ethnic minorities in the creation of independent media projects.

The workshop provided him with the opportunity to be around other people of color, filmmakers of color, and young people, like himself, who wanted to voice their opinions, often for the first time, through film and video. Randy got his hands on cameras and production equipment for the first time and started making short movies.

During his stint with Third World Newsreel, he directed *Cow Tipping: The Militant Indian Waiter* (1991) and *Haircuts Hurt* (1992). *Haircuts Hurt* is a short film about a Native woman who takes her long-haired, ten-year-old son to a barbershop for his first haircut. It was shot in the Lower East Side of the city in a predominantly Puerto Rican neighborhood. As Randy explains it, the set was dressed with a Confederate flag in the window to make it look like a redneck barbershop, because the film is about racism in the South.

When local residents saw the Confederate flag, many gathered out front to protest. Randy had to stop filming and run outside to explain that he was shooting a film and the flag was only a prop. That calmed everyone down.

Randy Redroad on location during a film production.

Shortly afterward, Native actor Irene Bedard (page 1)—the future voice of Disney's animated *Pocahontas*—moved to New York City to begin her acting career. She'd heard there was a Native American director in the city and wanted to work with Randy. She and Randy became friends, and, for a while, they worked at the same restaurant waiting tables, the kind of work many aspiring actors and filmmakers do to pay their monthly bills.

In 1994, Robert Redford's Sundance Institute offered Randy a spot in their Directors Lab, which takes place in June each year. This lab provides inexperienced filmmakers an opportunity to direct a few scenes from a script they've written. Guidance and advice come from experienced actors and directors with proven track records. Out of three thousand applicants, fewer than ten filmmakers are chosen for the lab each year. Randy brought a script titled *High Horse* to work on during the lab, and Irene Bedard was the primary actor who performed in scenes from that script.

After the Directors Lab experience, Randy returned to New York to shoot the whole film, in which Irene played the part of a Native woman. According to Third World Newsreel, which released the film, *High Horse* is a "provocative narrative film exploring the concept of home for Native Americans living in the city."

Descriptions of that project appeared in the book *Wiping the War Paint off the Lens*, written by Beverly Singer and published in 2001. The book tracked the progress of Native filmmakers who, in the 1980s and 1990s, were beginning to create filmed stories about Native peoples, an activity that had largely been dominated by non-Native filmmakers.

Singer wrote that Randy's film, which is filled with symbolic images, actions, and dialogue, portrays "dislocated Native people who search for and reclaim what has been stolen from the past in different journeys of loss, love, and identity."

Randy remembers that in those days it was hard to get access to filmmaking equipment, so with a grant from the New York State Council on the Arts, he and his production partner bought a 16mm film camera and field recorder. That was a very empowering move for them. It felt revolutionary, as though they were arming themselves to talk back to mainstream society and speak for themselves to audiences who had never heard Native voices.

A few years later, Randy was able to direct his first feature film, *The Doe Boy*, which is a very personal account about his relationship with his Irish-German father and their first deer hunt together. In the movie, partly based on an actual life event, the boy had a license to hunt and kill a buck but instead accidentally killed a doe.

However, Randy admits that he exaggerated the significance of the actual events in order to create a dramatic tale for film. "Once people in your life become characters in a story," he says, "it stops being the truth as you lived it and becomes the truth as the story needs it to be told in order to work as drama."

He entered *The Doe Boy* in the 2001 Sundance Film Festival and won the Sundance Film Festival/NHK International Filmmakers Award. He then went on to win thirteen other awards from film festivals and competitions. All those awards basically meant the film was an artistic success.

However, everyone knows that movies and documentary films cost money to produce. What everyone doesn't know is how to find the money to cover that cost. In the case of *The Doe Boy*, the director says it started with a letter of recommendation from internationally famous actor and director Robert Redford, who is the founder of the Sundance Institute.

That recommendation helped Randy obtain some of his first funding. Additional financial support came when the movie won the Sundance Film Festival award, because that particular award also included a cash prize of two hundred thousand dollars.

"My cinematographer, Laszlo Kadar, was also one of the film's investors, which is absolutely unheard of," Randy says. "So the money came together in a very special, unconventional way."

In spite of the film's awards and positive reviews, it never earned enough income to pay back all of the investors' money. That's not unusual for the movie business. It's disappointing to directors, producers, and investors alike, but out of the hundreds of feature films produced each year, a majority of those don't recover all of their production costs. Still, Randy considers *The Doe Boy* as his foundational feature film that provided him with a creative basis for future films. It put him on the filmmaking map, so to speak.

For the next couple of years, Randy worked with Yvonne Russo, Kimberly Guerrero (page 37), and the Akatubi Film and Music Academy, which focuses on teaching young Native Americans about the entertainment industry and new media (digital) production. As a result, he traveled a lot to Indian reservations and communities to teach filmmaking to Native youth.

Randy says the purpose of the program isn't just to turn kids into filmmakers but to also show them that they are worthwhile and that their thoughts are meaningful, have value, and can be shared with others. His involvement with the Akatubi Film and Music Academy was before the days of social media—Facebook, Instagram, or Twitter—so there were no real platforms of visual expression that Native youth had access to.

"No one can stop you from saying what's on your mind or keep you from getting your voice out there," Randy says. "That's very important for young people to know. Whether it's in life or business—having conversations with other people is really all we have. Those conversations can lead to agreements and to additional conversations, which could be job interviews or discussions to produce a movie. But believing you have something of value to contribute to those conversations is what makes you want to get up each morning and go out into the world."

Randy says the time he spent with the Akatubi program, working with people who became close friends and traveling to reservations and creating inspiring films with Native youth, was very fulfilling. It was during that time he realized he needed to reconnect with the West and get out of New York.

Those experiences allowed him to broaden how he defined himself as a filmmaker. He saw that being a film storyteller could take many forms, not just as a director. To survive financially, the reality was that he had to become proficient in all the filmmaking skills he could—writing, directing, producing, and editing—and be able use those skills as part of a team with a common goal.

Randy spent several years doing just that—performing different production tasks on a variety of documentaries and short films—until another turning point came while he was working on a project with husband-and-wife team Kimberly and Johnny Guerrero. Their task was to produce a short film for the Coeur d'Alene tribal community in Idaho. The content was to be about historical trauma, a very real problem that many Native American communities are trying to recover from.

We Shall Remain, the powerful and poignant music video they created, was posted online in 2014 and rapidly went viral. The song's lyrics, presented from a young Native girl's point of view, asks why so many Native parents today are addicted to alcohol or drugs or are mostly absent from their own children's lives. The answers, coming from the girl's uncle, tell the painfully true story of the suffering of generations of Native people at the hands of colonizing conquerors. Many of the dysfunctional behaviors of contemporary Indigenous people are the result of this history, causing pain and suffering generations later in a condition called historical trauma.

After *We Shall Remain* had been viewed thousands of times on YouTube, the creators decided to come up with a name for their production team that they could use for future projects; hence the name StyleHorse Collective was coined. Randy worked on certain projects as part of the collective, but for other projects, he worked on them as an independent contractor. This is still true today.

A few years later, Randy was asked by his friend Gilbert Salas (page 97) to help edit a movie titled *Edge of the World*. It was a contemporary story set on a West Texas horse ranch for boys. Gilbert was an experienced cinematographer and was the director of photography for the film. While shooting the movie, Gilbert saw firsthand the problems the project was having on location on a daily basis.

Based on Gilbert's recommendation, Randy met with the film's director to see about possibly editing the movie. Randy and the director didn't hit it off right away, and initially he declined to work with her. He gave her several ideas about how to fix the problems with the film's story and then went back home to Los Angeles.

Randy on location in Texas, directing the feature film *Edge of the World*.

Later, the director had a change of heart and offered Randy an excellent pay rate to edit the film. Eventually he agreed to come on board. One reason he agreed was that he knew Gilbert wanted this project to have a good outcome. Another reason was that the people at the horse ranch also really cared about this film. Randy felt that he wanted help their dream come true.

As the editor, he began sending notes to the director, telling her what was needed and how to shoot scenes in order for the story to work properly. The film's producer, who also knew the story line was in trouble, found that the director was throwing away all of Randy's helpful notes. Five days later, the producer fired the director and hired Randy to take her place and finish the movie.

"Gilbert and I made the best film that we possibly could," Randy says. "I'm really proud of the work we did there. I think it was the best job I ever did on any project up to that point."

Randy continues his filmmaking career on two fronts: creating and directing his own original pieces and taking on work-for-hire projects for which he's a member of a team.

The process of creating and directing his original pieces is an intensely personal experience.

"The shortest distance between the starting line and the finish line of a project is when it comes straight from the soul, the heart," he says. "In many ways, I still see the world through my West Texas lens, the lens of the experiences I had as a kid. That's where I learned about reality and dreams, lies and truth. Those things still drive my creativity."

SELECTED FILMOGRAPHY

2019: *The Infiltrators* (feature film); editor

2018: *Edge of the World* (feature film); director, editor

2015: *Wind Walkers* (horror movie); editor

2012: *Won't Back Down: A Tribute to Teachers* (short documentary); editor

2010: *First Circle* (documentary); producer, editor

2007: *Out of the Blue* (documentary); producer, editor

2003: *Moccasin Flats* (short film); director

2001: *The Doe Boy* (movie); director

1995: *High Horse* (short film); director

1992: *Haircuts Hurt* (short film); director

Gilbert Salas

INDIGENOUS MEXICAN-AMERICAN CINEMA-TOGRAPHER, DIRECTOR OF PHOTOGRAPHY

G ilbert Salas is an award-winning cinematographer and director of photography living in Los Angeles and working all over the world. He shoots everything from national TV commercials and short films to documentaries and features. Keenly aware of his own Indigenous roots, he has also been involved in several productions by and about Indigenous peoples since his earliest days in the business.

Gilbert was born in 1959 in El Paso, Texas, near where Mexico, New Mexico, and Texas intersect. His grandparents took part in the Mexican Revolution of 1910 to 1917, and their descendants fought for America in World War II and Vietnam.

"Our community wasn't downtown," Gilbert says. "We lived along the Rio Grande River. It was dirt roads, no sidewalks, adobe

Gilbert Salas.

and cinder-block houses. Where we lived was a lot like living on a reservation."

He was only four years old when his parents moved to Los Angeles so his father could find work. But his summers were spent back home with his grandparents and the rest of his family, which included many artists and musicians. He says the summer road trips between LA and El Paso taught him how to be mobile and adventurous, qualities that he now regularly puts to good use.

Gilbert credits his mother with preparing him for a life of storytelling and filmmaking. In their daily life, she often provided him with historical, social, and cultural contexts for the things he witnessed or experienced. Whenever a piece of music from another era came on the radio, she often explained how it related to the lives of his own parents or grandparents.

And she loved movies.

He remembers one Sunday morning when his grandmother dropped him and his mother off in front of the church. His mother waited until the elder had driven out of sight before explaining where they were actually going. Instead of walking into the church, they went down the street to see a movie.

"As I grew, I realized that I couldn't sit in a schoolroom and listen to a teacher," Gilbert says. "I just wasn't cut out for that, so I didn't prepare for college."

Instead, after high school he began doing odd jobs—temporary positions that didn't last very long. He was learning a variety of skills, but employers weren't eager to hire someone who changed jobs frequently. They wanted someone who could stick with one thing.

Finally, Gilbert landed a job as a swimming pool cleaner. During the day, he could enjoy his own thoughts while he cleaned people's backyard pools, and at night he could go to the movies or to music concerts.

One day he saw a classified ad in the newspaper: a photography studio needed someone to run errands, assist with props, and build sets. To Gilbert, this sounded like being in an art class, and art had been one of his favorite subjects in school.

He applied for the job, but the studio didn't hire him then. However, he felt that one day they might. So every few weeks he called back to see if they had any openings. And that persistence finally paid off about six months later, when he called and, for the first time, they asked him to come in to work on painting and building part of a set.

Because he'd paid attention in high school art classes, he already knew how to do what needed to be done for that job. They wanted him to paint a "cyc" (short for "cyclorama") background, build a platform, and construct a giant papier-mâché boulder. He finished the tasks in half a day, which was less time than a previous worker had taken to do similar work. So they asked him to come back the following day.

This time they sent him to a television production studio as an assistant. Upon seeing all the cables, lights, and equipment being set up by countless people who were running around chaotically, Gilbert felt right at home. He was able to step right into the workflow and figure out how to do what needed to be done.

And that, unexpectedly, was the beginning of his career in film and television production.

Gilbert continued to work for that production company for two years, learning on the job. To him, it was like going to film school. There he learned the basics of lighting and sound recording, how to work with actors, and which techniques would help ensure a smooth and successful outcome.

That's also where he learned the importance of networking, which is the process of interacting with others to exchange information and develop professional contacts. Gilbert believes this is a vitally important part of working in the entertainment industry. It's also the way to learn about new production projects that could very well become your next paid gigs.

Gilbert spent much of his time during his twenties learning a variety of production-crew jobs, including the duties of grip and gaffer, both of which play critical roles in large-scale productions.

A grip's job is to operate equipment that moves and supports cameras. This includes tripods, dollies, tracks, jibs, cranes, and stationary rigs. A gaffer is the chief lighting technician and the head electrician responsible for the execution of the lighting plan for a production.

"One thing I noticed is that crew people on movie sets really love their jobs," Gilbert says. "When you're doing something you love that is unique and exciting, you pay attention to what's going on, and that keeps you on your toes and healthy."

Gilbert thinks working in the film industry is somewhat like joining a circus. As long as you have a little bit of drive, curiosity, and willingness to try different things, there's a way to get into the business. Plus, there are more opportunities than ever with the growth of streaming services, such as Netflix, Amazon Prime Video, Apple TV, and hundreds of cable TV channels.

Many years ago, Gilbert narrowed the focus of his work to the camera department. He started at the bottom of that area of production and worked his way up to the top. That top position is the director of photography, someone who works closely with the director.

The director is in charge of the whole vision of the project and knows the story and how it should be told. The job of the director of photography, DP for short, is to help the director visualize that story and to determine what kind of camera and media to use.

Depending on the size of a project and the number of people working on it, the director of photography may also be the camera operator. On large-budget projects, they are two different people.

Under the director of photography is a set of crew members that includes the first and second assistant camera operators. These two make sure that all the camera gear and recording media are ready to go, all the batteries are charged, and

Gilbert Salas on location as director of photography, shooting a feature film.

the lenses are standing by. They ensure that whatever the DP might need is handy and ready for use.

In the days when movies were shot on motion-picture film, the process was very straightforward. The same system had been used for decades. Since the transition from film to digital media, some aspects of the job are more complex because various types of digital cameras use different systems to electronically record images and sound.

Another complexity within the entertainment industry is the contrast between union and nonunion projects. Decades ago, production personnel began forming unions so that movie producers wouldn't take advantage of workers by making them work long hours with low pay.

The union that protects camera operators is the International Alliance of Theatrical Stage Employees. Gilbert joined this union in the 1990s because it allows him to work on film and TV productions that are considered union jobs. Films that use union personnel cost more to produce and have more rules to be followed.

"There are a lot of rules on union projects," Gilbert explains, "but there are a lot of benefits as well, because there is a guaranteed level of expertise a producer can count on. Because a producer may be hiring expensive actors, they need production crews that can get the job done quickly and expertly. Crew members benefit from rules that prevent producers from asking them to work too many hours each day."

Gilbert works on union as well as nonunion productions and enjoys both.

"Sometimes production budgets are so small that they can't afford to pay for higher-cost union personnel," Gilbert says. "A good group of creative crew members can work together flexibly and still produce a high-quality product at a lower cost."

One of the projects Gilbert is most proud of is a documentary television series called *Storytellers of the Pacific*, which was broadcast on PBS stations in 1996. Teams of mostly Native filmmakers documented the impact European colonization had on the Indigenous peoples of the islands and coastal regions of the Pacific Ocean. Choctaw producer-director Phil Lucas supervised that international joint effort for the US production team.

"I traveled to Hawaii and Samoa to shoot segments on how colonization affected Indigenous languages, cultures, and identities," Gilbert says. "We interviewed contemporary Native peoples to learn about what they're doing now to bring back their cultures that had almost been destroyed by European intrusion and control."

A few years later, Gilbert was fortunate enough to have what he calls the experience of a lifetime filming *Sailing the Master Home*, a short film documenting a month-long ocean voyage on a traditional Pacific Islander outrigger sailing canoe. Using a small digital video camera, Gilbert became the primary cinematographer for what he considered to be a "dream project" when the original camera operator became sick.

A particular master sailor of the Polynesian culture had just spent twenty years among the Hawaiians, teaching them the ancient Indigenous method of sailing across the ocean without the use of maps or compasses. A grateful sailing community of Native Hawaiians was returning the elder to his home community several thousand miles away.

"I got to sail with them for a month, and we took him right to his home island," Gilbert says. "The film was shown at the Smithsonian Institution in Washington, DC, and then at the Sundance Film Festival. It was a wonderful opportunity to connect my own Indigenous identity to a larger sense of what it means to be Indigenous."

For Gilbert, the most important factor in becoming successful in the entertainment industry, or in any business for that matter, is how you view yourself. In the early days of his career, he was often the only "brown guy," to use his term, in a room full of white guys.

"It could be a little intimidating, and it was," Gilbert says. "I had to have talks with myself to remember that I'm one of the people in this room who can get the job done. If there's a problem that needs solving, I can figure out a solution."

He says that you can't look at yourself as a brown person and the other person as white. "You have to learn to look at the group as just a set of people trying to figure something out. If you happen to come up with an idea or a solution, they will forget that you're that brown person who just walked in. You simply become a useful member of the group."

At that point, according to Gilbert, you can work on a challenge together, and if you're successful in meeting that challenge, you get to do it again, and again, and again. In that scenario, you've allowed yourself to believe that your input is valid and your contribution is worthwhile. From his perspective, self-esteem and self-confidence play huge roles in being successful in work and in life.

Gilbert believes that a large part of understanding who you are is how you come to define your own identity. Part of that identity includes what community you come from or what community you feel a part of. The color of your skin can be a factor in self-identity too.

"Whether I'm in Los Angeles, El Paso, or Mexico, I can be treated differently by different groups of people based only on the color of my skin," Gilbert says. "In Mexico, they call me Indio, which means 'Indian.' In Los Angeles, people call me Mexican. Either way, I know I'm a person of Indigenous roots from the Tarahumara Indian people. I've come to understand that the term 'Chicano' applies to a person like me. Chicanos are people of Mexican descent who are proud of their Indigenous roots and who celebrate those roots."

Gilbert states that becoming comfortable and confident in who you are allows you to walk into a room and go to work with whomever else is in that room. "If someone doesn't like the color of your skin or the nationality they think you come from, it's not your problem. It's their problem."

SELECTED FILMOGRAPHY

2018: *Edge of the World* (feature film); cinematographer

2017: *House of Tomorrow* (feature film); camera operator

2014: *Johnny Geronimo: Renaissance Indian* (short film); cinematographer

2013: *Dark Skies* (feature film); camera operator

2005: *Trudell* (feature documentary); cinematographer

2003: *Sailing the Master Home* (short documentary); cinematographer

1996: *Storytellers of the Pacific* (TV documentary series); cinematographer

1993: *Body Snatchers* (feature film); first assistant camera operator

1991: *The Dark Wind* (TV movie); assistant camera operator

1990: *Emperor of the Bronx* (feature film); second assistant camera operator

1989: *Cannonball Fever* (feature film); first assistant camera operator

Ian Skorodin

CHOCTAW WRITER, PRODUCER, DIRECTOR

Born to a Choctaw mother and Jewish father in the mid-1970s, this writer, producer, and director has been a positive, dynamic force within the Native filmmaking community. His directing credits include several productions that explore his mixed cultural roots, but his selfless efforts have improved the overall status of Native filmmakers within the Los Angeles–based entertainment industry.

His father was a doctor from Chicago, who went to work for the Indian hospital in the Choctaw Nation of Oklahoma. There he met and married Ian's mother, who was a nurse at that facility. A few years after Ian was born, the family moved to Chicago, where the boy started attending synagogue and going to Hebrew school on Sundays.

Every summer, the family returned to Oklahoma to visit Ian's mother's side of the family and reconnect with her Choctaw roots.

Ian Skorodin.

Ian vividly remembers what first sparked his interest in being a filmmaker:

"When I was nine years old, I saw the gangster movie *Once Upon a Time in America*," he says. The four-hour film is about a prohibition-era Jewish gangster and his buddies in New York City. "I was just blown away by the whole thing," Ian continued. "The experience of going to the movie theater, seeing a four-hour movie with an intermission—I wanted to make movies ever since I saw that."

When he graduated from high school, Ian enrolled in film classes at the University of Oklahoma, where he learned the basics of filmmaking and produced short films. After two years, he transferred to New York University's Tisch School of the Arts and eventually earned a bachelor of fine arts degree in cinema.

While in a screenwriting class at Tisch, Ian wrote a movie script called *Tushka*, the story of the murder of the family of a Native American political activist. Then, during summer breaks back in Oklahoma, he directed the feature film, which he completed in 1996.

After premiering at the Sundance Film Festival in 1998, *Tushka* went on to win Best Feature Film at the Arizona International Film Festival and the Spirit Award at the First Nations Film Festival in Chicago. Two years later, the film secured distribution for both US and international audiences.

After finishing film classes at NYU, Ian moved to Oklahoma, where he produced a documentary for the Choctaw Nation's archives about its original tribal enrollees. Then came a short stint as a news videographer for a station in Tulsa.

Ian soon moved to Los Angeles, which was always part of his long-range plan, and began looking for work. In the year 2000, Native American Public Broadcasting Consortium (now Vision Maker Media) hired Ian to shoot video in LA as part of a documentary about that year's election. He was shooting a press conference at the Staples Center downtown that was also being covered by Univision, a Spanish-language TV station. Being friendly, Ian began chatting with the Univision crew about shooting video. A week later, someone from Univision called him and asked him to do some freelance work. That led to an offer for a full-time job with the station as a video news photographer.

What impressed Ian right away was the enormous jump in his pay rate. The Oklahoma TV news job paid about eight dollars an hour, but the LA news job paid him thirty-six dollars an hour!

One thing that really benefited Ian when he moved to LA was just being friendly to people he worked with. Even though he didn't speak Spanish, many Univision reporters liked to use Ian to shoot their news pieces because it gave them a chance to practice their English. Their goal was to eventually go to work for the mainstream English-speaking news channels, because those jobs paid even more.

During his early years in LA, Ian produced his own short films and took on freelance production work to make a living. He says it's not unusual for filmmakers just starting out to take on side jobs like bartending to pay bills while they are trying to get production work. That's exactly what he did.

One of the projects he originated in the early 2000s was an animated short film he called *Crazy Ind'n*. He says it was something he worked on in his spare time because "it was fun to do." According to Ian, it's "the story of one Native's quest to reclaim a stolen artifact and right a great injustice" in a world where Native peoples are taking back their lands through military force.

He entered *Crazy Ind'n* in imagineNATIVE, a Canadian film festival. Personnel from Canada's Aboriginal Peoples Television Network (APTN) saw the film during the festival and asked Ian if he would be interested in making it into a series. APTN was established in 1992 to create and broadcast programs made for and about the Indigenous peoples of Canada and the United States. APTN bought the first episode of *Crazy Ind'n* and paid Ian to produce others.

The original episode was screened in England, Finland, and New York, and won Best Animation at the Cherokee International Film Festival.

In addition to this ongoing project, Ian began producing documentary and educational videos for tribes. He says that was a rewarding experience and provided an opportunity to learn more about other tribes.

However, he realized he really wasn't making any progress toward his main goal, which was to get involved in LA's entertainment industry and work with the studios and networks based there.

He also realized that LA's Native community of actors and filmmakers really wasn't connected to the industry either. That's why he decided to create a Native film festival in Los Angeles in 2007. He hoped it would eventually help provide Native people better access to all aspects of the entertainment

Ian Skorodin preparing for a production workshop for Native youth.

industry. He formed a nonprofit organization with a board of directors and named it the LA Skins Fest.

Having entered a few festivals as a filmmaker himself, Ian had some ideas about what a good festival needed to have to benefit Native filmmakers: a good venue, a good audience, and additional opportunities beyond just screening films. The world-famous Sundance Film Festival, for example, was attended by movie distributors who were looking for films to circulate to theaters and audiences across the country.

Ian points to the pioneering efforts of Mike Smith (1950–2018), who created the American Indian Film Institute and the American Indian Film Festival in 1975, the first film festival created to specifically show Native-made documentary and narrative films. That festival, now held in the fall in San Francisco, includes a lavish awards show where the winners in several categories receive beautifully sculpted awards. Once held in the prestigious Palace of Fine Arts, the event gives filmmakers and actors a strong sense of validation for their work.

"A lot of us, well, myself and a few others, probably wouldn't have a film festival if Mike Smith hadn't done it first," Ian says. "He inspired us to do something to help make Native filmmakers and actors more visible to audiences and to the industry."

The LA Skins Fest, coproduced by Indigenous filmmaker Patricia Gomes, started out as a small annual event that screened Native-made films, but it didn't have a permanent home. With little or no funding, it bounced around from venue to venue for the first few years.

While planning and running the film festival, Ian still continued to produce short films. One such project was *Walking on Turtle Island*, completed in 2009. This was a pilot episode for a proposed television series set in the Old West, starring Tantoo Cardinal (page 9) and Saginaw Grant. It premiered at the Ashland Independent Film Festival in Ashland, Oregon.

Then Ian directed *The Homestead*, a firsthand account of the Choctaw survivors of the Trail of Tears in the 1830s.

Next came a historical documentary for and about the Ramona Band of Cahuilla Indians in Southern California.

In between other projects, Ian developed the feature film *Ten Little Indians*, which is about Native people in prison. As if that didn't keep him busy enough, he also directed several music videos for a number of bands, including a Native blues band called Native Roots.

Then, in 2011, the Autry Museum of the American West invited the LA Skins Fest to hold the event in their in-house theater, which boosted the festival's public visibility. But the ultimate goal was always to hold the festival's film screenings in an actual movie theater, and that finally became a reality for LA Skins Fest in 2015 when it moved to the TCL Chinese Theatre on Hollywood Boulevard. Since Hollywood is often thought of as the entertainment capital of the world, it was the perfect place for the festival to be located.

Ian wasn't finished with creating opportunities for Native actors and filmmakers to get noticed by the industry, though. In addition to the film festival, LA Skins Fest went on to host workshops for Native actors, directors, and writers. The workshops weren't just held during the festival. LA Skins Fest began hosting monthly sessions year-round in which Native people could hone their skills and hear from experienced entertainment professionals.

In 2016, Ian established the Native American TV Writers Lab as a platform for Native writers to launch careers in television writing. That was followed by the creation of the Native American Feature Film Writers Lab, which had a similar objective of training Native writers to create scripts for movies.

As the LA Skins Fest grew year to year, Ian was able to establish working relationships and sponsorships with many entertainment giants, including Sony Pictures, CBS, A&E Networks, United Talent Agency, HBO, Paramount Studios, and the Walt Disney Company.

Ian's work as a filmmaker and film festival director has given him insights he shares with others. For instance, he thinks it's important for more Native people to get involved in the industry at some level.

"When people think of getting involved in the entertainment industry, they first think of the glamour and fame, or being in front of the camera," he says, echoing the advice of Michael Horse (page 47). "But there are so many more opportunities behind the camera in terms of writing, directing, shooting, and editing. And there are also even more jobs as grips, makeup artists, wardrobe, props, and set people, and a lot of other positions that work on shoots daily."

Ian teaching camera technique to a Native youth.

According to Ian, people of all ages have misconceptions about the production business.

"You don't ever really 'make it big' in the entertainment industry the way people think," he says. "For most people, working in this field is made up of a series of short-term jobs. All anyone really ever has is the current job, the project they're working on now. When that one ends, you have to find the next one, and the next one."

He says that you may land a really big job that pays well and keeps you working for a long time. But then when it's over, you may only be able to find a small short-term job the next time. Nothing's for certain.

"You have to have realistic expectations and understand that it takes commitment," he says. "It can take a decade to build a good, solid career. It doesn't happen overnight."

He stated that some people think it might take them a year to break into LA's entertainment industry, but it can take a year just to figure out how to drive to the places you need to go in the city. And it's a major challenge for many Native people to move from their home community to Los Angeles. It takes financial resources. And once you're in LA, you have to work hard to find work. There are so many people already there, some with more education and experience.

"But if you're talented in some way, you might have a chance," he says. "If an opportunity comes your way, you have to be ready for it, show your best work, and do your best job. Then you'll be asked to do it again on another project."

Now might be a good time to give it a try, because there's a big push for diversity in the industry these days. Now is a good time to be writing scripts, making short films, and getting them out there to be seen.

"Industry executives are looking for diverse new voices," Ian says. "So if anyone makes a film, they can always enter it in the LA Skins Fest."

SELECTED FILMOGRAPHY

2016: *Bitch Please* (TV series, 2 episodes); director

2015: *Wave: Part 2* (short film); writer, director

2014: *Wave* (short film); writer, director, editor

2014: *Jew in Choctaw Country Part 2*; writer, producer, director

Jew in Choctaw Country Part 3; writer, producer, director

2013: *Jew in Choctaw Country* (short film); writer, director

2012: *Crazy Ind'n Part 4*; writer, producer, director

2010: *Escaped* (short film); writer, director, editor

Crazy Ind'n Part 3; writer, producer, director, editor

2009: *Walking on Turtle Island* (short film); writer, director

2007: *Crazy Ind'n* (animated short); writer, director, editor

Crazy Ind'n: The Sequel (animated short); writer, producer, director, editor

1996: *Tushka* (feature film); writer, director

Academy Award: The name given to the prestigious film awards presented each year since 1927 by the Academy of Motion Picture Arts and Sciences (AMPAS), a professional organization for those engaged in the production of motion pictures. Each award, often referred to as an Oscar, is for international recognition of excellence in cinematic achievements as determined by the Academy's voting membership.

"Action!": The word called out by the director at the start of a scene's filming to alert actors to begin performing.

Actor: Refers to any male or female who plays a character role in a movie, television program, stage play, or other production; alternate gender-neutral terms include: "player," "artist," or "performer."

AFTRA: Stands for the American Federation of Television and Radio Actors, a union created to protect the rights of television and radio actors.

Animation: A process of filmmaking in which inanimate, static objects or individual drawings are filmed frame-by-frame (one frame at a time), each one differing slightly from the previous frame. This is done to create the illusion of motion in a sequence.

Call Sheet: A type of schedule given out periodically during a film's production to let every department know when they are supposed to arrive on the set and where they are to report. This term often refers to a listing of actors necessary for a particular scene.

Camera Angle: The position chosen from which to film or photograph a subject. Various camera angles, compositions, or positions include front, behind, side, top, high (looking down), low (looking up), eye level (standard, or neutral, angle), tilted, and subjective.

Cast: A collective term for all of the actors and performers appearing in a particular film or play. The cast is often separated into two groups: (1) the leads and the supporting characters with speaking roles, and (2) the background players, or extras, and the bit players.

Character: The fictitious or real individual in a printed or filmed story, portrayed by an actor on-screen.

Cinema: Another word for "movies" or "motion pictures."

Close-up (CU): A camera shot taken from a close distance in which a person or object appears relatively large and fills most of the frame to focus attention on it and emphasize its importance.

Credits: On-screen text that lists the names of the people who worked on a movie or television program and their jobs. This includes the director, producers, camera crew, technical personnel, cast, production crew, editing personnel, and many others.

"Cut!": A word called out by the director to stop the actors from performing and tell the camera operator to stop shooting.

Cyclorama (or "Cyc"): A curtain or wall that forms a backdrop in a theater, or film-TV studio.

Dialogue: Any lines in a film or television program spoken by an actor, usually based on a written script.

Director: The person responsible for complete artistic control of all phases of a film or television production, including everything from guiding the actors' performances and supervising the cinematography to making costume, hair, and makeup choices.

Documentary: A nonfiction film, video, or television program that is unscripted and tells a true story about real events and people.

Editing: The process of selecting, assembling, arranging, trimming, structuring, and joining together many separate sounds and camera shots to create the final movie or television program.

Episodic TV: A scripted television series that feature episodes broadcast about once a week or streamed on a streaming service such as Netflix, Amazon Prime, Hulu, or Apple TV.

Feature Film: Another term for a movie or motion picture. It is more than sixty minutes in length and is usually about ninety to one hundred twenty minutes. These productions are still referred to as "films" even though actual film is no longer used.

Film Festival: An event during which films can be premiered, exhibited, and awarded. Often simply called a "film fest." The American Indian Film Festival, founded by Mike Smith, was the first film festival that screened and awarded films made by or about Native Americans.

Filmmaker: A general term used to refer to a person who has a significant degree of control over the creation of a film. This includes directors, producers, screenwriters, and editors, or individuals who may perform all those roles.

Filmography: A comprehensive listing of films featuring the work of a particular actor, director, or other crew member.

Gig: A job that lasts for a certain length of time and then ends. The term is used for many temporary work assignments, including acting and production-crew positions.

Hollywood: A district within Los Angeles. Also a term often applied to moviemakers as a whole who are based in the general Los Angeles area.

Live Action: The opposite of animation, this is the filming of naturally occurring action or live objects or people at a regular frame rate.

Movie/Motion Picture: See "Feature Film."

Pitch: In the film and television industries, "to pitch" means to present an idea or a project for consideration, such as an idea for a TV show or movie.

Postproduction: The finishing stages of a production project that take place after the shooting or filming has ended. This may include sound dubbing, sound-effects editing, picture editing, and so forth.

Preproduction: The planning stages in a film's production before the principal photography or actual shooting begins.

Producer: The person in charge of getting a movie or TV show made and who manages the production from start to finish. The producer is involved in various logistical matters (such as scheduling, financing, and budgeting). The list of tasks varies from project to project but may include raising funds and financing; acquiring or developing a story; finalizing the script; hiring key personnel for cast, crew, and director; and arranging for distribution of the film to theaters.

Public Broadcasting Service (PBS): A collection of television stations in the United States that are supported by donations from the viewing public and business sponsors.

Screen Actors Guild (SAG): The union formed to help protect the rights of actors. The organization negotiates with producers and directors to create rules about how actors are to be treated while working on a movie or TV production. Only about 5 percent of SAG members work often enough and make enough money to support themselves solely through acting.

Screenplay: A type of script (see below) used for filming a movie using a prescribed format as a series of master scenes, with all the dialogue provided and the essential actions and character movements described.

Script: The written text of a film, training video, informational film, or short film; a blueprint for producing a film that details the story, setting, dialogue, movements and gestures of actors, and the shape and sequence of all events in the film.

Showrunner: The leading producer on a television series who has the ultimate creative control and management responsibility. This person may also be one of the show's writers and has the power to fire and hire personnel.

Take: A single, continuously filmed performance. A shot or version of a scene with a particular camera setup. A director may shoot several takes of the same scene until all the elements of the scene come together in a satisfactory manner.

Aboriginal Peoples Television Network (APTN)

Headquartered in Winnipeg, Manitoba, this Canadian cable and broadcast network was created with government support in 1992. It produces and airs programs made by, for, and about the Indigenous peoples of Canada and the United States. Programs that have aired on the network include the documentary *Mohawk Girls*, the drama series *Moccasin Flats*, the animated series *The Deerskins*, and the music series *Rez Blues*. More information can be found online at aptn.ca.

Academy of Motion Picture Arts and Sciences

Also known simply as "the Academy," this professional honorary membership organization is known worldwide for its annual Academy Awards, or Oscars. Headquartered in Beverly Hills, the Academy's facilities are housed in three separate locations containing screening theaters, libraries, offices, and research centers. In recent years, several Native American actors and filmmakers, including Irene Bedard (page 1), Tantoo Cardinal (page 9), Bird Runningwater, Q'orianka Kilcher, and others, have been invited to join the eight thousand members of the Academy.

In 2019, Cherokee actor Wes Studi was honored by the Academy with an Oscar for portraying "strong Native American characters with poignancy and authenticity" in more than thirty films. Canadian Native musician Buffy Sainte-Marie shared the Oscar for Best Original Song in 1982.

American Indian Film Institute and Festival (AIFI)

Founded in 1975 by the late Michael Smith (Fort Peck Sioux), AIFI continues to be a major presenter of Native American media arts in California. The festival is the world's oldest and most recognized international film exposition dedicated to

118

Native American cinematic achievements. For more information, go to aifisf.com.

imagineNATIVE Film + Media Arts Festival

Based in Toronto, Ontario (Canada), this festival, founded more than twenty years ago, is a trailblazing platform for Indigenous storytellers. The event, held annually in October, continues to grow every year and aims to spotlight the diverse stories and traditions found within Indigenous cultures. To learn more, go to imaginenative.org.

LA Skins Fest

Founded in 2006 by Ian Skorodin (Choctaw; page 105) and Patricia Gomes (P'urepeche), this Native American film festival takes place in Los Angeles each November. Since 2016, the festival's films are screened at the TCL Chinese Theatre in Hollywood, but other festival-related events are held in different venues, such as the Netflix offices, SAG/AFTRA headquarters, and the Academy of Motion Picture Arts and Sciences. The organization also hosts effective year-round training events and programs for Native writers, directors, and actors. For more information, go to laskinsfest.com.

Native Cinema Showcase

Sponsored by the National Museum of the American Indian (NMAI), this annual festival takes place in New York City each March and then again in Santa Fe, New Mexico, during the Santa Fe Indian Market in August. Home base for the event is the George Gustav Heye Center, a branch of NMAI, which hosts the March festival. The Southwestern Association for Indian Arts (SWAIA) cohosts the August event, usually held at the New Mexico History Museum and other venues. For further information, visit AmericanIndian.si.edu and swaia.org.

On Native Ground (ONG)

Founded by filmmaker Jack Kohler (page 57), On Native Ground (ONG) is a media, film, and public relations company and a tribal nonprofit incorporated within the Hoopa Valley Tribe. ONG utilizes film and multimedia to promote cross-cultural understanding and positive visibility to tribal communities and tribal organizations. Their activities include youth training in media production as well as various full-scale productions for stage and screen. For more information about On Native Ground, go to onnativeground.org.

Santa Fe Native Cinema Film Festival

Held each February in Santa Fe, New Mexico, this festival takes place in conjunction with the Santa Fe Film Festival that began in the year 2000. For more information, visit santafefilmfestival.com/index/tag/native-american. To see what films showed in their 2019 festival, go to facebook. com/1623797404558658/videos/2006247489668475.

Sundance Institute's Native American and Indigenous Program

Founded in 1981 by actor-director Robert Redford, the Sundance Institute has supported Native American filmmakers with training and funding assistance and has also screened Native-produced film projects. Through fellowships and labs, Native filmmakers receive mentoring, guidance, and support in various aspects of filmmaking, including scriptwriting, directing, and producing. Find additional details online at sundance.org/programs/indigenous-program.

Vision Maker Media

Founded in 1976 as Native American Public Broadcasting Consortium by founding executive director Frank Blythe, the organization came into being to support the creation, promotion, and distribution of Native American media for public television and radio. Now, as Vision Maker Media, the organization continues to fund the development and production of programs about the histories, cultures, and contemporary issues of Native communities. For more information, go to visionmakermedia.org.

Michigan State University Libraries Research Guide. "Native American Studies Research Guide: Native American Documentary Films." Accessed June 11, 2020. libguides.lib.msu.edu/c.php?g=95603&p=624343.

Singer, Beverly R. *Wiping the War Paint Off the Lens: Native American Film and Video*. Minneapolis: University of Minnesota Press, 2001.

Page 4: Photographer unknown

Page 11: ABC's "Stumptown" stars Tantoo Cardinal as Sue Lynn Blackbird. (ABC/Matthias Clamer) © American Broadcasting Companies, Inc. All Rights Reserved.

Page 17: Photo by Katia Badalian

Pages 20, 23, 24: Photo by Alissa Banks

Pages 27, 28, 32, 35: Courtesy of Sydney Freeland

Page 37: Photo by Pamela Peters, Navajo Nation

Page 40: Photo by Shane Brown, Cherokee Nation

Page 43: Photo by Carrie Rosema

Page 48: Photo by Camille Seaman

Page 53: Photographer unknown

Pages 57, 59, 60, 64: Courtesy of Jack Kohler

Page 68: Courtesy of Wendy D.

Pages 71, 75: Photos by Tae Hoon Kim

Pages 77, 80, 83: Courtesy of Canadian National Film Board

Pages 88, 90: Courtesy of Randy Redroad

Page 95: Courtesy of Jaki Covington

Page 97: Courtesy of Gilbert Salas

Page 101: Courtesy of Jaki Covington

Pages 105, 108, 111: Photos by Patricia Gomes

Award-winning writer and filmmaker Gary Robinson (Choctaw/Cherokee descent) has participated in the production of more than one hundred educational, informational, training, and documentary television projects, primarily on Native American topics.

In 2015, Gary was presented with the Best Animation Award for his short film *We Are All Related* at the fortieth Annual American Indian Film Festival hosted by the American Indian Film Institute in San Francisco, California. He was the writer, producer, and director of the film.

Gary is the author of eight PathFinders novels: *Thunder on the Plains*, *Tribal Journey*, *Son Who Returns*, *Little Brother of War*, and the Billy Buckhorn Trilogy: *Abnormal*, *Paranormal*, and *Supranormal*. His novel *Standing Strong* is about a young water protector finding her path and dedicating her life to the greater whole.

Gary Robinson

Other titles by Gary Robinson include: *From Warriors to Soldiers*, *The Language of Victory*, and *Powerful Medicine* (a Johnny Geronimo mystery). He also authored *Native American Twelve Days of Christmas* and *Native American Night Before Christmas*, illustrated by Jesse T. Hummingbird. Gary lives in rural central California.

7th Generation publications celebrate the stories and achievements of Native people in North America through fiction and biography.

The **Native Trailblazer Series** for adolescent readers provides inspiring role models of Native men and women whose lives have had a positive impact in their communities and beyond.

For more information, visit:
nativevoicesbooks.com

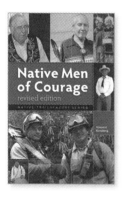

Native Men of Courage
REVISED EDITION
Vincent Schilling
978-1-939053-16-9 • $9.95

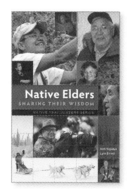

Native Elders:
Sharing Their Wisdom
Kim Sigafus and Lyle Ernst
978-0-9779183-6-2 • $9.95

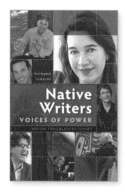

Native Writers:
Voices of Power
Kim Sigafus and Lyle Ernst
978-0-9779183-8-6 • $9.95

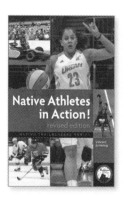

Native Athletes in Action!
REVISED EDITION
Vincent Schilling
978-1-939053-14-5 • $9.95

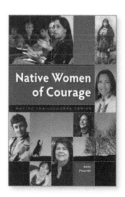

Native Women
of Courage
Kelly Fournel
978-0-9779183-2-4 • $9.95

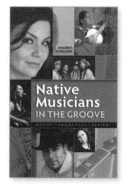

Native Musicians
in the Groove
Vincent Schilling
978-0-9779183-4-8 • $9.95

Available from your local bookstore, or you can buy them directly from:
Book Publishing Company ● PO Box 99 ● Summertown, TN 38483 ● 888-260-8458
Free shipping and handling on all orders.